A Rose Loupt Oot

Poetry and Song Celebrating the UCS Work-in

Edited by David Betteridge

Published 2011 by
Smokestack Books
PO Box 408, Middlesbrough TS5 6WA
e-mail : info@smokestack-books.co.uk
www.smokestack-books.co.uk

Printed by EPW Print & Design Ltd

ISBN 978-0-9564175-0-3
Smokestack Books gratefully
acknowledges the support of
Arts Council England

Smokestack Books is
represented by Inpress Ltd
www.inpressbooks.co.uk

This book is dedicated to the memory of
Jimmy Airlie (1936-1997)
and Jimmy Reid (1932-2010),
and to all the other shipyard workers of UCS
and their allies,
who, in 1971-72,
made a historic stand
and saved their yards from closure.

'A reading of history implies a shared taking into consideration of events, their causes and their consequences, a discussion about the possible margins of manoeuvre (history is seldom generous), and then the presentation and explanation of a policy. Promises made without this are all delinquent... I recall a sentence by Anton Chekhov: "The role of the writer is to describe a situation so truthfully... that the reader can no longer evade it." We today with our lived historical experiences, which the political machines are trying to erase, have to be both that reader and writer... it's within our power.' John Berger, 'Erasing the past', *The Drawbridge*, August 2007

Acknowledgements

'The Freedom Song', 'God Save the Shipyards', 'Has Anybody Here Seen Kelly?', 'Let Him Go, Don't Let Him Tarry', 'U.C.S.', 'Under Heath There's Nothing for Us' and 'United All' are located in Glasgow Caledonian University's research collection archives (Communist Party of Great Britain file). Thanks are due to Willie Thompson for permission to reproduce them here. Freddy Anderson's 'Ballad of the Red Clyde' is held among this poet's papers in the same university archives. Thanks to Paul Anderson for permission to reproduce it here.

Acknowledgements are due to Third Party for permission to reproduce the lyrics of Matt McGinn's 'Wi' Jimmy Reid and Airlie' and 'Yes, Yes, U.C.S.', with thanks also to Janette McGinn for her permission. The following lyrics appear here with the permission of the songmakers and/or their publishers: Danny Couper's 'A Shipyard on the Clyde', Dick Gaughan's 'Keep Looking at the Light', Iain Ingram's 'The Final Ship', Arthur Johnstone's 'Doon Through the Years', Danny Kyle's 'The Great Iron Ship', Tony McCarthy's 'The Death of the Clyde', Jimmie Macgregor's 'Pack Your Tools and Go', Geordie McIntyre's 'Writing on the Wall', and Jim McLean's 'Head Teeth'. Thanks are due also to Eddie and Leanne Coyle for permission to reproduce their father Leo's 'Song o the Yard' and to Janey Kyle for her father Danny's 'The Great Iron Ship'. Every effort has been made to trace the copyright holder of Tony McCarthy's 'Death of the Clyde', but with no success. Any information on this score would be gratefully received, to set the record straight in future editions.

Thanks are due to Carcanet for permission to reproduce 'Glasgow Sonnet V' from Edwin Morgan's *Collected Poems* (1996). Thanks are due also to the authors and their publishers for the following poems: Jim Aitken's 'Struggle', first published in *Glory* (Clockwork, 2001), and 'Redemption' in *Being Beneath the Moon* (Magdalene Press, 2008); Jackie

Kay's 'The Shoes of Dead Comrades', first published in *Off Colour* (Bloodaxe, 1998); Tessa Ransford's 'Counting', first published in *Not Just Moonshine* (Luath Press, 2008); and Brian Whittingham's 'The Titan Crane', first published in *Bunnets and Bowlers* (Luath Press, 2009). Bill Sutherland's three poems from *A Clydeside Lad*, are reproduced here, with thanks, by permission of Catherine Sutherland and Clydeside Press.

The following poems were written specially for this book: Jim Aitken, 'Clydebuilt'; David Betteridge, 'Banner and Roses', 'Jaggily' and 'Showing a Way'; Alistair Findlay, 'Clyde-built: the UCS' and 'The Industrial Relations Act, 1971'; Donna Franceschild, 'Something Like Grief'; Danny McCafferty, 'Fresh Chapters'; George McEwan, 'Ballad for Upper Clyde'; Aonghas MacNeacail, 'an còmhlachd / in unison'; Chrys Salt, 'He Wouldn't Want an Elegy'; Peter Scrimgeour, 'I See the Salmon Flow'; Gerda Stevenson, 'I Am the *Esperance*'; Brian Whittingham, 'At the UCS Work-in'.

Acknowledgements are due to West Dunbartonshire Libraries and Museums Service for permission to reproduce photographs of theirs on pp 39, 46, 52, 60 and 62, and on the book's front cover. Ken Currie's 'Sketch for Panel 7 – The UCS' is reproduced courtesy of Culture and Sport Glasgow (Museums). Thanks are due to Ken Currie himself for permission to reproduce his 'UCS' drawing, currently on display in the STUC offices in Glasgow. Thanks, too, to Owen McGuigan for permission to reproduce his photograph of the Titan Crane on p80.

Contents

Preface

Ann Henderson

The poems, songs, words and images gathered here will bring back memories for some people, and serve as an introduction to the UCS work-in for others. Either way, it is an opportunity to reflect, to listen and to be inspired. The lives of so many families and communities in Scotland have been shaped by the shipbuilding industry. The struggles in the early 1970s belonged to those families, but also to the wider labour movement, in the rest of the UK and internationally.

Poems and songs were an integral part of getting the message out. At concerts, speeches, rallies, and marches, more and more voices were brought together, and, most importantly, they were heard.

Men, women and children came together to fight for the right to work, for the right to be treated with respect, and for a society that could provide for all.

Thousands of workers came out to join huge demonstrations in Glasgow in June and August 1971, including the women from Glasgow's cigarette factories and from Singer's of Clydebank, who marched alongside the men from the shipyards.

Ten years later, in 1981, women workers occupied the Lee Jeans factory in Greenock, successfully saving jobs and preventing a multi-national company withdrawing funding. 'It was the first time that a crowd of women and girls had done it. The Govan shipyards had done something a bit similar a few years before but they were all men.' [1]

The action taken by the UCS workforce in the 1970s ensured hope and work for thousands of workers and their families. Apprenticeships, skills and engineering expertise are still being passed on.

1: Ina Anderson, 'Fighting for Our Jobs: An Account of the Lee Jeans Sit in', in Shirley Henderson and Alison Mackay (eds) *Grit and Diamonds: Women in Scotland Making History 1980-90* (1990).

But also we must revive those campaign skills, energy and co-ordination, and the legacy of a movement which put people before profit.

The story of UCS cannot be told without that of the STUC. In August 1971, the STUC convened a special Congress, going on then to host a wider Committee of Inquiry into the social and economic consequences of the disastrous policies being pursued by the Conservative Government. In October 1971, the STUC brought together an Assembly on Unemployment, leading the discussions on the specific economic problems facing Scotland.

Today, the STUC finds itself again seeking to give voice to our families and communities facing unemployment, as the future of the welfare state, public services and any remaining industry in Scotland is again under threat.

With an uncomfortable resonance for today, Angela Tuckett, in her record of the first 80 years of the STUC (1897-1977), wrote: 'With the return of a Conservative Government under Ted Heath in the summer of 1970, a tremendously heavy work load for the STUC developed as they moved into a period of years of industrial strife.' [2]

Take the time to enjoy the words, images and music in this book. Sharing our history must bring strength and optimism for the future and that is what we need, if we are to do justice to those who have gone before.

Ann Henderson is Assistant Secretary of the STUC. She has responsibility for liaising with Government and Parliament, and serves as Secretary to the STUC Women's Committee.

2: Angela Tuckett, *The Scottish Trades Union Congress: The First 80 Years* (1986).

A Truly Historical Event

Jimmie Macgregor

The events of 1971/2 on Clydeside were undoubtedly the most dramatic and inspirational in recent Scottish working class history. Under sympathetic management and a Labour government, the shipyards had been steadily climbing out of the doldrums, and things looked promising. A change of government soon changed that. When Edward Heath's administration, with its inbuilt horror of public ownership, announced, almost off-handedly, that the Upper Clyde consortium of major yards were to be forced to the wall, the reaction, not only on Clydeside, but all over Scotland, was one of shock and disbelief. The potential consequences for thousands of families and for the Scottish economy as a whole have been too well rehearsed by experts to require any further comment from me.

I am a child of industry. My Dad supported us by sweating his life away in a steelwork which made Dante's inferno look like a rest home. I grew up in Glasgow when the city built things. There were foundries and blast furnaces. We had railway works, shipyards and steelworks, and, to paraphrase one of Jimmy Reid's more colourful phrases, the city also built men: men whose labours had made them physically tough, and as the Heath government was to discover, mentally tough too. These were people who were proud of a huge range of skills, and who created the biggest man-made moving objects on the face of the earth.

As the full potential of the impending calamity was realised, resistance grew and supporters of all kinds rallied round. Tony Benn, articulate as ever, lent his considerable political weight, and Bob Fleming, Provost of Clydebank, authorised funding to take delegates to London. There were contributions from small businesses, from clergymen, shopkeepers and countless individuals. Collecting boxes appeared everywhere, and top Scottish entertainers swelled the funds with sell-out concerts.

Even the folk fraternity pitched in with an album called *Unity Creates Strength*. My own contribution to that was a song which I called 'Pack Your Tools And Go.' I had a line which said 'Along came a man whose name was Reid.' I later changed that to 'There was Gilmore, Airlie, Barr and Reid', but realising that even that did not credit all the people who were involved, I reverted to the original version, leaving Jimmy Reid's voice to represent everyone else. A song was a modest enough contribution, but I am grateful to have been involved, however marginally, in a truly historical event which demonstrated the courage, resilience and basic humanity of ordinary working people.

We Said No

Jimmy Cloughley

The UCS campaign has been described as the most innovative and significant victory for workers in the last century. It was led by Jimmy Reid and Jimmy Airlie, remarkable men and both communists, supported by Sammy Barr, Bob Dickie, Willie McGinnes, Bob Cook, Gerry Ross, Davie Torrance, Sammy Gilmour, Bobby Starrett (UCS cartoonist), Roddy McKenzie, Davie Cooper and other shop stewards and convenors who were running various sub-committees at Upper Clyde Shipbuilders.

In the Seventies, there was massive unemployment in Scotland, with factory after factory facing closure, or closing. Shipbuilding was in decline. Very few shipyard workers knew the benefits of full-time or regular employment. A key date in the industry was The Geddes Report of 1966. This was a wide-ranging report on shipbuilding. Its main recommendation was the grouping of the shipyards, the result of this being the formation of the Upper Clyde Shipbuilders (UCS) in 1968, under a Labour government.

Then in 1969 a secret Tory strategy to do down UCS was drawn up by Nicholas Ridley. This infamous Ridley Report said, No more public money to UCS. Let Yarrow leave UCS if they want to. This will lead to the bankruptcy of UCS. We shall then put in a government butcher to cut up UCS, and sell cheaply the assets of UCS to Lower Clyde and others. After liquidation or reconstruction as above, we shall sell the government holdings of UCS, even for a pittance.

The Ridley Plan has been described as the Lowland Clearances. It was a step-by-step plan to undo UCS. The later report (1970) of the 'Four Wise Men' appointed by Edward Heath's Tory government coincided not only in detail but in almost every dot and comma with Ridley. The four men were Alexander McDonald, Chairman of Distillers; Sir Alexander Glen, a shipping magnate; David MacDonald, a merchant banker, of Hill Samuel; and Lord Robens. They did not inspire those at UCS with confidence. As Jimmy Reid stated, it virtually meant the death knell of the upper reaches of the Clyde. UCS was being sacrificed on the altar of sheer political dogma. Its closure would have disastrous social and economic repercussions on the West of Scotland, in terms of unemployment, not only in shipbuilding but in all ancillary industries.

Our resistance to this proposed butchery was the work-in of 1971-72, the first campaign of its kind in the history of trade unionism. 'We are not going on strike,' Reid explained. 'We are not even having a sit-in strike. We are taking over the yard, because we refuse to accept that faceless men can make these decisions. We will conduct ourselves with dignity and discipline... The shipyard men at UCS are not wildcats. They want to work. The real wildcats are in 10 Downing Street. The biggest mistake we could make would be to lie down, capitulate and grovel.'

This speech launched a massive response to the campaign, and goodwill flowed in. Later in 1971, the secret Ridley Report was unveiled by Reid to a special meeting of the Scottish Trades Union Congress (STUC), called to discuss the social and economic consequences of closing UCS. It was dynamite.

On August 16th, 1971, the Scottish TUC called a special Congress for the first time in its history, to address its grave concern about the Scottish economy. Jimmy was invited to speak for the UCS shop stewards. 'It is time,' he said, 'that the working class wrote a charter of rights, at the heart of which would be the right to work. If the government cannot guarantee that right, and if the social system cannot guarantee that right, then we must change the Government or modify the system.' The delegates expressed their enthusiasm for the fight at UCS by giving him a standing ovation.

At the final mass meeting of the UCS work-in, on 9th October, 1972, when it was clear that the government had been forced to change its policy, and that all the constituent yards of UCS would remain open, Jimmy wound up the proceedings by saying, 'What we're reporting here today is a historic achievement for you. All these people that told us over 15 months it couldn't be done, they will not craw today. We will let the facts speak for themselves... We will make publicly known our sincere appreciation to these millions of working men and women, throughout the length and breadth of this country, that enabled us to continue. It's as much a victory for them as it is for us.'

The UCS campaign in 1971 and 72 showed that working men and women, given principled leadership and information, can make decisions about their work and their communities that are in the best interests of those communities. Yes, we all walked taller then. Confident, inspired, we grew in stature. We said No to the destruction of our communities, refusing to stop work, and organising ourselves into a highly efficient workforce, instead of meekly accepting the economic and political facts of life, and joining the dole queue. It happened here on Clydeside. It applies equally today.

Today we say goodbye to Jimmy Reid, a Scottish legend, lost to the nation. A passionate man, an intellectual, a polymath, a prophet; a nationalist and internationalist, he drew people to him. He loved them, and they in turn trusted him. He was not afraid to voice his opinion against authority, the state, institutions, or individuals in it. He considered it his duty, a hero and champion of the people.

I'll finish by quoting Burns, who captures this vision: 'Whatever mitigates the woes or increases the happiness of others, this is my criterion of goodness; and whatever injures society at large or any individual in it, this is my measure of iniquity.' Good- bye, Jimmy.

Abridged from the eulogy given at the funeral of Jimmy Reid, at Govan Old Parish Church, 19 August, 2010. Jimmy Cloughley, a friend of Jimmy Reid's, was an engineering shop steward in the Govan Division of UCS, and headed the Publicity Committee of the UCS Co-ordinating Committee during the work-in, along with Davie Torrance, Drawing Office shop steward.

Drawing by Ken Currie

Introduction

David Betteridge

The idea for this book came from Bob Starrett, whose cartoons leap so strongly from its pages. Forty years ago, these same cartoons added their sharp comment to the pages of another publication, a series of *Bulletins* issued by the shop stewards and convenors of the Coordinating Committee of UCS. These *Bulletins* documented the progress of that remarkable episode of history-in-the-making, the UCS work-in of 1971-72.

At the time, UCS was often in the news. Later, regrettably, it became less well known, even to the point, in some quarters, of being confused with a clothing store in Clydebank. What sort of history is being taught and learned if the name and achievement of the work-in at Upper Clyde Shipbuilders is allowed so to fade? It was here, in that consortium of yards, that the then government's plans for shipbuilding on the Clyde were successfully opposed by the action of the shipbuilding unions, joined by numerous allies. This action took the form of a 'work-in', a new term for a new form of resistance. Bob Starrett, a shipyard worker and an artist, lived through all the debates and decisions and actions that led to the government being forced at last into a policy U-turn, and the yards being saved from their intended closure. What might we do, Bob Starrett wondered, to celebrate the 40th anniversary of this achievement? Our publisher, Andy Croft, of Smokestack Books, specialises in poetry, so it was poems that he wanted on the subject, and songs, plus, of course, Starrett's cartoons, along with whatever illustrations and bits of prose might help to contextualise them. Readers may like to regard this resulting book, *A Rose Loupt Oot*, as a kind of large and lyrical birthday card, with many signatories.

We began to compile our anthology in July, 2010. The work proved to be a delight, and up to a point easy, given the volume of goodwill and practical help available on request. Early in the process, George Kerr (a shop steward in Yarrow's at the time of the work-in) along with Arthur Johnstone (a founder member of The Laggan, and lynchpin of the Star Folk Club) and the editor (a long-time friend of Bob Starrett) joined forces in a visit to the treasure trove of Glasgow Caledonian University's research archives. There Audrey Canning, Carole McCallum, and Philip Wallace gave us the benefit of their knowledge, both of the political songs and other resources that they held, and of the people and campaigns that produced them. We went away with a good haul of material.

An appeal for more material and for tip-offs regarding other likely sources was placed in the *Morning Star*, and then emailed to a long list of friends and colleagues. As well as old songs and poems, we wanted new ones, to add to Arthur Johnstone's fine five-verse contribution, written specially for the book at the very outset, 'Doon Through the Years', to the tune of 'Nicky Tams'. Aonghas MacNeacail rose to the occasion, contributing an heroic poem, 'an còmhlachd /· in unison'. Over the succeeding weeks and months, Jim Aitken, Donna Franceschild, Danny McCafferty, George McEwan, Peter Scrimgeour, Chrys Salt, and Gerda Stevenson also contributed new poems, all interestingly different; and other poets (and/or their publishers) agreed to their previously written works being included, too. See the editor's Notes (below).

An important ally in the editorial process was Ewan McVicar (singer, songmaker, storyteller, author, teacher, publisher). His encyclopaedic familiarity with the folk-song scene, and its ramifications into wider aspects of cultural and political life proved invaluable. From the start of the work-in, folk singers and songmakers supported it, performing at marches and rallies, and organising benefit concerts. Jim McLean produced a record, *Unity Creates Strength*, anthologising songs relevant to the campaign, and donated the proceeds from its sale to the UCS fighting fund. We have included notices for some of the concerts as illustrations, and have provided the lyrics for a selection of the songs that were written and sung at the time: songs by Danny Couper, Danny Kyle, Matt McGinn, Jimmie

Macgregor and Jim McLean. We even have half a dozen work-in songs by Anon, and about the same number of songs written later, which reflect on the legacy of the work-in from a variety of standpoints. Ewan McVicar's Notes (below) tell their story in detail.

Ken Currie (whose series of *History Paintings* in the People's Palace powerfully recount the Labour Movement's progress over two centuries) gave permission for us to reproduce a large black-and-white drawing of his, commemorating UCS; it currently hangs in the STUC headquarters in Glasgow. Accompanying this drawing, we include a preparatory sketch for the seventh of the *History* paintings, also commemorating UCS. Bob Starrett drew some new cartoons for use as section headers in the book, basing his work both on his memory of the yards and on picture research done at Glasgow Caledonian University. John Foster (co-author with Charles Woolfson of the magisterial *The Politics of the UCS Work-in*) undertook to provide a Further Reading list, for those of our readers who want to pursue in prose the questions that the songs and poems and cartoons collected here may provoke. Jimmy Cloughley (publicity convenor for UCS at the time of the work-in) agreed to abridge and adapt the eulogy that he gave at Jimmy Reid's funeral in August, 2010. It provides a valuable insider view of the work-in, grounded in experience and engagement. John Berger gave permission for us to take a slightly tinkered-with extract from a recent essay of his, *Erasing the Past*, and use it as a motto text, our endeavour being, like his, the opposite of erasing, namely remembering. Ann Henderson, of the STUC, undertook to write a Preface for the book. In it, readers will see just what a volume of support the work-in received, and how relevant to today's struggles similar broad alliances are. Jimmie Macgregor, well-known as a singer, author, broadcaster and long-distance rambler, contributed a memoir, 'A Truly Historical Event'. Here he sets the work-in in the context of history, and shows the prominent role played by songs, his own included.

Our search for material continued apace in a welter of communications that would require a complex diagram to illustrate, such as is used by chemists to show the linkages of big molecules. (George Kerr's mobile phone was central.) Looking for the photographs that we wanted proved especially long-drawn-out, entailing phone calls, emails, letters, and visits to more than a few libraries and museums. Pat Malcolm, Jo Sherrington, and Trish Robins, at Clydebank Reference Library, and Mark Nixon, at Clydebank Museum, went beyond the call of duty to steer the editor's research. Our front cover design, which shows a very eye-catching UCS banner being carried through the streets in a demonstration, would not have come into being without their help in tracking down a photograph, now in Clydebank Reference Library's picture archive, taken by Alex Young.

Other photographs relevant to our theme, but far too numerous to include here, were discovered by searching the internet. Two websites in particular repay close study. The University of Glasgow Archive Services www.archives.gla.ac.uk hold a picture record of the history of John Brown's, including that yard's famous building of the *QE2*. Then there is Owen McGuigan's splendid gallery www.myclydebankphotos.co.uk showing several decades of Clydebank life. We are indebted to him for the photograph of The Titan Crane that we use to contextualise Brian Whittingham's poem of the same name, and Danny McCafferty's 'Fresh Chapters'. This photograph shows the crane in its present role as a tourist attraction, towering above a flattened and rebuilt riverside environment. To the photographer, as to others, the crane is 'just a large tombstone to the death of Clydebank's shipbuilding'. To others, it stands as a proud icon of Clydebank's regeneration. Which interpretation is right is for our readers to decide. Owen McGuigan was also of assistance in bringing to our attention the songs of Leo Coyle, recorded on a CD called *Clyde Born*, one of which we include here, 'Song o the Yard'. Thanks are due to the songmaker's son and daughter, Eddie and Leanne, for permission to publish it. The whole of *Clyde Born* can be enjoyed on Owen McGuigan's website. There is also a short film featuring 'Song o the Yard' on YouTube, accessible on the same website, and held in the Scottish Screen Archive. In its range of thought and feeling, the film encompasses much the same as this book, but in a nutshell.

Our work on the book was soon overtaken by the death of the best-known figure associated with the work-in, one of the UCS Coordinating Committee, Jimmy Reid. His funeral, on 19 August, 2010, attracted a great deal of public mourning and media coverage, and served to bring the events of 1971-72 back into the arena of debate. One outcome was the good news, announced at the funeral by the First Minister, Alex Salmond, that Learning Teaching Scotland would provide and promote curricular resources relating to Jimmy Reid and the UCS work-in, for use in secondary schools. Of course, to conflate the man and the work-in, as some news commentators did, is to misunderstand both; but credit where credit is due, we thought, in coming to our decision to include Jimmy Reid's name in the book's dedication. After all, as well as playing an important role in the collective leadership of the work-in, as did Jimmy Airlie, another dedicatee, he served as one of its most persuasive spokespersons. Later, he went on to write memorably about it, in language that resounds. This being a book that celebrates the work-in *in* language, we could not avoid being drawn towards his force field *of* language.

We are aware that there are readers who evaluate Jimmy Reid's life less than favourably. Some, including friends of his, regret his decision to leave the Communist Party and join the Labour Party; and some regret his decision to leave the Labour Party and join the Scottish National Party. (Others recognise a consistency of allegiance – to certain principles, if not to parties – in these moves.) Some regret the fact that journalism of his appeared in Rupert Murdoch's *Sun*, believing that Reid miscalculated when he thought that his left-wing spoon was sufficiently long-handled for supping with that particular right-wing devil. (Others point out that he never trimmed his words to suit the paper's editorial policy. He wrote *in* the *Sun*, not *for* it.) A hard-argued debate about these rights or wrongs will go on, and so it should, if lessons for the future are to be learned, with no distortion or erasure.

We are aware also of what Jimmy Reid himself called the 'great man' or 'swashbuckling Errol Flynn' way of looking at events, which is a fallacious way. 'There is a capitalist concept of history,' he said, in a speech he gave on Communism (1966), 'which sees history as the story of outstanding individuals... It consigns the great mass of the people to a spectator role.' This concept is clearly wrong, so, in naming Jimmy Reid as one of the book's dedicatees, we place him fair and square in the tradition of the Labour Movement struggles that preceded him, and of which he was a product; and fair and square in the collective leadership of the UCS work-in. Jimmy Cloughley's 'We Said No' makes very clear this tradition and this collectivity of leadership.

We continued our networking and our trawls through the summer and into the autumn and winter of 2010, landing the catches that readers can now, we hope, enjoy. Just as the first original contribution to the book was a song, Arthur Johnstone's 'Doon Through the Years', so was the last: a call to political action from the standpoint of the tragedy of the Miners' Strike of 1984-85, the very negation of 1971-72. This was Dick Gaughan's strong and inspiring 'Keep Looking at the Light', set to an original tune, conceived as 2010 came to its frozen end, amid all manner of bad news from the economic, political and social fronts of Britain and the world. By then, regrettably, our book's success rate had begun to diminish – certain trails of enquiry went cold, and certain fault lines of opinion opened up – with the result that, as it stands, the book is not as broad in its spectrum of views as we had intended. It contains too few women's voices, and too few contributions from an internationalist standpoint. Our spectrum of views would have been even narrower had it not been for the compensatory efforts of George Kerr, Jimmy Cloughley, Carol McCallum, and, latterly, of Danny McCafferty, active in West Dunbartonshire politics, and currently chairperson of an anti-poverty initiative in Clydebank. Thanks are due to them for commissioning and collecting some of the short prose comments, or 'witness statements' as we came to call them, that occur throughout the book. They cast their net wide, as we wanted to hear, not only from 'big names', but also from the extraordinary 'ordinary people' whose support for the work-in ensured its success. Their comments, combined with some quotations from published sources, add a valuable freight of lived experience and interpretation to the events of 1971-72. We have interspersed them with our songs and poems.

In William Morris's great utopian novel, *News From Nowhere*, there is a chapter where the time-travelling narrator meets Philippa and a group of her fellow stone-masons. They, the Obstinate Refusers, decline to join in the hay-making celebrations that the other citizens go off to. Nowhere would be less instructive as a fictional place without their principled dissent. To quote another radical, one of Morris's great predecessors, William Blake: 'Without contraries is no progression.' Not surprisingly, given its determination to celebrate the UCS work-in, our book is short of certain 'contraries'. Its starting premise and direction of travel made it uncongenial to those who deny that the work-in was an important demonstration of workers' power, and deny that it is worth celebrating. It follows that our readers must go elsewhere to complete their survey of 1971-72. They may choose to look, for example, at an article by Steve James, posted on a website maintained by the International Committee of the Fourth International just after Jimmy Reid's death. There they will find a thorough-going negation of much of what this book celebrates. The article contends that, 'Through the "work-in", the UCS dispute became synonymous worldwide with the promotion of class compromise and reformism in a militant guise... [It was] decisive in diverting a powerful movement in the working class away from a fight to bring down the then Conservative government of Edward Heath.' Clearly, Blake's 'mental fight' cannot be avoided.

Other editors, then, starting from different premises from ours, will be able to offer more than we can, engaging wider constituencies of poets, songmakers, and informants. Other editors, and their publishers, may also decide to look into genres of writing additional to poetry and song. There is drama to enjoy, notably Frank Miller's *Work-in* (part of the CRAN Theatre Group's *Govan Trilogy*), and *The Great Northern Welly Boot Show* (co-written by Billy Connolly, Tom Buchan, and others), the first being epic and documentary in

Drawing by Ken Currie

its historical details, the second being comic, and at a satirical tangent to real events. There are memoirs, too, and speeches, and political studies, and miscellanies e.g. Martin Bellamy's wide-ranging *The Shipbuilders* (2001): a sufficient shelf-load of publications to keep this one, *A Rose Loupt Oot*, company.

Readers who want to investigate the politics of the work-in in some depth will find John Foster's 'Further Reading' at the end of the book a useful starting point. Those whose interests relate primarily to songs in the context of their times can turn to two books by Ewan McVicar, *One Singer One Song* (1990), and *The Eskimo Republic* (2010). His Notes prefacing our selection of songs give a taste of these books' riches. See also Ian Watson's sociologically probing *Song and Democratic Culture in Britain* (1983), *The People's Past* (1980), edited by Edward Cowan, *McGinn of the Calton* (1987), by Matt McGinn and Janette McGinn, *Alias McAlias* (1992), by Hamish Henderson, and *The Democratic Muse* (1996), by Ailie Munro. Singers in search of the tunes for the songs that we have collected have a wide choice of sources to turn to, electronic as well as print. See Ewan McVicar's list of sources at the end of his Notes. It should be pointed out that, in the case of our two songs that are set to original tunes, namely Iain Ingram's 'The Final Ship' and Dick Gaughan's 'Keep Looking at the Light', we have included the tunes' notation alongside the lyrics. Thanks are due to Dick Gaughan for applying his computing skills to the task of notating his own song, and to Chris Sennett for adapting it to fit the new dimensions of our page; and thanks, too, to Eddie McGuire (composer and performer, in whom West has dialogue with East, and classical music has dialogue with folk) for copying Iain Ingram's 'The Final Ship' in his own clear hand.

Readers whose interests relate primarily to poems might turn to Hamish Whyte's Introduction to his jam-packed anthology of verse about Glasgow, *Mungo's Tongues* (1993), or to David Craig's chapter on 'The Radical Literary Tradition' in *The Red Paper on Scotland* (1975), a far-ranging collection of essays brilliantly edited by the (then) young and (then) left-wing Gordon Brown, later to achieve a different kind of eminence.

Other relevant works are *A History of Scottish Women's Writing*, by Douglas Gifford and Dorothy McMillan (1997); *The Tears that Made the Clyde*, by Carol Craig; and Christopher Whyte's *Gendering the Nation* (1995). To set these authors' insights in their still living historical context, readers will find no better guide than John Foster's chapter on 'The Twentieth Century, 1914-1979', in *The New Penguin History of Scotland* (2001), edited by R.A. Houston and W.W.J. Knox. Teachers looking for resources relating to the Clyde, and shipbuilding, and/or the events of 1971-72, are well served by a number of agencies. They may turn to Clyde Waterfront or Clydebank Rebuilt, or to Learning Teaching Scotland, under whose aegis resources are being considered which will be in accordance with *A Curriculum for Excellence* guidelines.

Our book's title, *A Rose Loupt Oot*, may puzzle some readers, but not those who are well versed in Hugh MacDiarmid's *A Drunk Man Looks at the Thistle*. There, in a passage about the General Strike of 1926, the poet (or his persona in a ditch) describes seeing a symbolic rose 'come loupin' oot' after ages of running to waste, 'Wi' pin-head flooers at times.' But this time, the rose erupts into bloom, and grows and grows until 'It was ten times the size / O' ony rose the thistle afore / Had heistit to the skies.' Indeed, it seems as if the whole world has turned into a 'reid reid rose that in the lift / Like a ball o' fire burned.' The parallels between 1926 and 1971 seemed to the editor and publisher worth highlighting in this literary choice of title of ours. Following MacDiarmid, we are looking beyond the often prosaic and messy details of political action to its potential, its promise, its 'hidden hert o' beauty.'

To summarise: many, many thanks are due to all those collaborators and contributors whom we name above, and those whom we do not have space to name, who helped to convert Bob Starrett's starting idea into the paper and print of *A Rose Loupt Oot*. They did so for no personal gain, this book coming as it does from a no-profit, no-wage publishing house. They are to be thanked, but not held responsible for any deficiencies in the finished product. Responsibility for those lies with the editor. Errors of fact and of style, legion to start with, have been greatly reduced along the way by the sharp eyes and sharp wits of the editor's daughter, Hazel Betteridge. Thanks are due also to all those who buy this book, and read it, and enjoy it, and ponder how powerful the combined action of people can be when they are united, and are well led in a just cause, and how powerful language can be, whether in speeches or written articles or songs or poems, in serving to mobilise action. Especial thanks will be due, above all, to those who learn from the example of the UCS work-in, and continue its tradition of struggle, probably in new forms, in new times.

During the work-in, before its outcome could be predicted, the novelist Archie Hind wrote a piece of reportage for *Scottish International*. He allowed himself 'a fantasy', as he called it:

> *that one day a ship would be permanently berthed on the Clyde, as in the Cutty Sark at Greenwich and the Queen Mary in the States. In front of the gangway would be a notice, or plaque, which would say: 'This is the first of a long line of ships built by UCS workers at John Brown's shipyard in defiance of a reactionary government, permanently berthed here to commemorate and honour those same workers who brought life back to British socialism'.*

A fantasy, yes; and also unfinished business.

Notes on the Songs and Songmakers

Ewan McVicar

The River Clyde flows through Glasgow's heart. The old saw says 'The Clyde made Glasgow and Glasgow made the Clyde', because the emerging city deepened the river so that sea-going ships could come right up to the quays of the Broomielaw, and from this flowed much trade and the building of ships along the river's banks.

Songs in general praise of or comment on the river and its people were made. The music hall 'Song of The Clyde' tells of leisure travel 'doon the watter' to the resorts, Paul Joses' 'My Song of The Clyde' of journeying by train from Dumbarton to Glasgow along its banks. Another music hall favourite, 'Sailing Up the Clyde', made by Will Fyffe (a Dundonian), celebrates return from abroad, while the children's playsong 'Wha Saw the 42nd?' tells of the 42nd Highland Regiment marching down the Broomielaw to enship for foreign service. The Broomielaw features in several song accounts of courting or of drunken misadventures, and more humour features in 'I love the lassies, ah'm gaun tae wed them aa, when the broom blooms brawly on the bonny Broomielaw', and in an account of a drunken day trip to Rothesay that took place when New Year's Eve was in the middle of July – 'Wan Hogmanay at the Glasgow Fair'.

Some of these folk and music hall songs of the 19th and earlier 20th Century were much sung in the early 1950s days of the Scottish Folk Revival, and when song enthusiasts gained confidence in their own ability to recycle tunes and make new lyrics, the life of the River featured strongly. Songs were made in sarcastic praise of the 'sludgy boats' which took Glasgow's waste down river to dump it in the Firth of Clyde. Glasgow's best-known songmaker of the Revival was Matt McGinn. His song in praise of Glasgow boxer Benny Lynch says 'The whole of the river sang "Benny has been"', and McGinn brings a 'Big Orange Whale' swimming up the Clyde to play football for Rangers. Shipyard engineer Jim Brown wrote of the freighter

'The Western Trader' steaming up the Clyde, and the last of the pleasure paddle-steamers 'The Waverley' rolling down the river. Iain Ingram met and unsuccessfully courted Annie McKelvie while 'oot walkin alang the Clyde shore'. Billy Connolly sang of 'Doon at Saltcoats furra Fair'.

New songs of the Folk Song movement were set in the shipyards. An early entrant, in the late 1930s, was Ewan MacColl's rewrite of a Peninsular War ballad of fallen Scots soldier 'Jamie Foyers', in which Foyers lays down his tools and goes from 'the shipyard that stands on the Clyde' to fight and die in the Spanish Civil War. In his 1960s 'Propeller Song', Jim Brown tells of a revenge punishment by shipyard gaffer Charlie Provan. Matt McGinn weighed in with 'The Ballad of the *Q4*', the name while under construction of the liner that was then christened the *Queen Elizabeth*, 'Can o Tea' about a shipyard strike, and 'The Welder's Song' in which the yard worker is thinking on his beloved.

When Glasgow folk song activist and politician Norman Buchan wished to write a song about the yards for a BBC radio series called *Landmarks*, he enlisted singer Archie Fisher to collaborate on the lyric, and fiddler Bobby Campbell to compose the tune, for 'The Shipyard Apprentice'. Appropriately, both Fisher and Campbell had, like several other Revival singers, most famously Billy Connolly, begun working life as yard apprentices, only to be turned away when their apprenticeship time was up and there was no adult job available to them. Fisher says only his own verses are in the version that is given in this book, though this is disputed by Buchan's widow Janey. The song has proved enduringly popular, but with the changing fortunes of the Clyde yards other songmakers, Alasdair Robertson and John McCreadie, have both made their amended versions of the narrative.

When the UCS work-in commenced, Danny Kyle amended his song 'The Great Iron Ship' on the building of the liner *Queen Elizabeth* on Clydeside in the 1960s. His final verse had advised the young apprentice to 'get out with the tide', but he changed it in his final chorus to 'please hang around and fight from inside'. Matt McGinn, Jimmie Macgregor, Jim McLean, Danny Couper and one or more unidentified hands wrote new lyrics for old familiar tunes to be used directly at the UCS support demos and marches, some of them specifically about the work-in, others more general political assaults.

In the years after the work-in, songwriters Iain Ingram, Geordie McIntyre, Leo Coyle and Tony MacCarthy all wrote laments for the loss of the yards. What was the purpose of the songmakers? Political songmakers do not expect to change the political opinions of the uncommitted or opposing listener. They rather aim to express their outrage or determination, to support approved of action, to simply articulate feelings and principles, to recount examples of approved or deplored actions and incidents, and, in the case of the songs made specifically to be used at demos, they sought to create their own tools that could support the struggle.

This was in part a habit of the times – folk singers were very active at Scottish political rallies in the 1960s. A famed and much admired precursor of the UCS songs was the early 1960s songmaking and singing campaign of the Eskimos to support and articulate the aims of the anti-Polaris demonstrations at Dunoon in the Firth of Clyde. The key architects and song creators of the Eskimo approach were Morris Blythman and Jim McLean, but Matt McGinn and a dozen more contributed songs, verses or lyric ideas. The makers carefully utilised warmly familiar tunes, so the songs could be grasped and passed on the more easily. For the same purpose, the songs created for use during the work-in also all adopt known tunes and strong clear choruses, while, for those written before or after the work-in, the maker has usually composed a new tune and at times has eschewed any chorus.

In part the songs arose from an enduring Scots habit of commenting in song on political issues. Scots songbooks before and after Robert Burns hold a few favourites still employed for support of political causes of the left or right, and many more lyrics to known tunes that were surely explosive in their day, but their specific references to then current issues and personalities make them opaque in meaning now. And of course the enduring favourites tend to have stronger poetic qualities and to be more generally applicable to social issues than those left behind. Burns himself penned a few still sung, and many then topical political squibs that went bang and left their empty shells behind. He too did not compose new tunes, though he often adapted tempi.

Turning now in detail to this book's selection of UCS songs and their makers, **Danny Kyle** was very well-known as a folk performer, broadcaster and organiser, and his 'Great Iron Ship' had the distinction of being played as part of a landmark radio series, John Purser's BBC Radio Scotland series *Scotland's Music*. Purser commented that Danny's song harked back 'to earlier times, for the days of riveters' guns playing tattoos on the hull were over, replaced by the spark and zzzip of welding – a wonderful sight at night, with blinding flashes of colour from all directions, briefly illuminating some improbable shape in the dark. Work went on 24 hours, of course.'

Another very well-known broadcaster and singer, **Jimmie Macgregor**, made a song specifically to celebrate the work-in. Jimmy Reid wrote in 1977 that 'folk music has no meaning unless it expresses the lives and struggles of ordinary people. Future historians seeking a true understanding of our times will look to the school of protest song, and not to the palliative products of commercial pop. Robin Hall and Jimmie Macgregor do not receive the full recognition they are due for their contributions in the folk music field. In 1971, when the shipyard workers on Upper Clyde refused to accept the butchery and dismantling of their yards, it was inevitable that the folk song world would give it expression. It was equally inevitable to me that Robin and Jimmie would be involved. Fund raising concerts were organised, and all the artists' services were without payment. A number of songs were written, and among the best was Jimmie's "Pack Your Tools and Go." It requires no explanation, the hallmark of all good protest songs.' Robin and Jimmie were for 21 years the best known performers of Scots folk song.

Photograph by Alex Young

The next best known Scots singer and songsmith in the folk song field in the 1960s and 70s was **Matt McGinn** – he topped the bill at New York's Carnegie Hall one evening, while far down the bill was a polite young man called Bob Dylan. Astonishingly lyrically able and prolific, Matt spilled new songs out at such a rate that many were off his performing list again before they could be recorded. Neither of the two songs in this book was included in his autobiographical *McGinn of the Calton*, both lyrics being the kind of populist squib he could dash off then deliver with roaring demotic elan. Both songs, and several others made and sung by McGinn, can currently be found on the Internet as sound partners with YouTube sequences of film and still photos, evoking the atmosphere of the work-in or of bygone scenes of Glasgow. The spirit of elation that political song in its rightful place can arouse is shown in a photograph in *McGinn of the Calton*. Matt, Danny Kyle, Billy Connolly and his then Humblebums partner Tam Harvey, and others salute the crowd and themselves.

Jim McLean's name is far less familiar, yet he penned the lyrics for many songs for the cause of Scottish Republicanism and the anti-Polaris campaign, when he was a key member of the Eskimos, and then, as a record producer he organised many key commercial recordings. His best known lyric begins 'Oh cruel is the snow that sweeps Glencoe, and covers the grave o' Donald.' McLean's UCS lyrics are more developed than McGinn's short punchy songs. 'Head Teeth' neatly, satirically and incisively skewers PM Edward Heath. His tunes are carefully selected so that knowledge of each original lyric further sharpens his stiletto. 'Head Teeth' talks about the workers' actions, and its energetic American tune 'Casey Jones' is about a noble tragic railroad engineer. 'Cowes Capers' (not included here) lampooned Heath's much publicised 'messing about on the Channel' on his yacht, utilising the tune of the 1960s popular song 'Messing About On The River'.

While Kyle and McGinn were based and active in Clydeside, McLean sent his song contributions up from London, as did **Tony McCarthy** with his sadly defeated 'The Death of the

Clyde', with a note written on the songsheet, 'I hope this song is useful'. McCarthy was active in editing CND songsheets and singing in London folk clubs, but I've been unable to learn much more about him. **Danny Couper**, who sent his song 'A Shipyard On The Clyde' down from Aberdeen, is more defiantly angry and determined, and his employment of the tune and atmosphere of Burns' call to battle 'Scots Wha Hae' backs up his insistence on the need to fight. Couper is still a politically committed folk song activist and singer in Aberdeen.

What about other songs made to support the struggle? I am sure that more songmakers, not traced by us during our work on this volume, made and sang songs in local folk clubs at the time. We did uncover the clutch of six **'Anon'** songs that we include, discovered in the Research Collections of Glasgow Caledonian University's archives. Thanks are due to the archivists, Carole McCallum and Audrey Canning, for their great help here, in delving into the voluminous Gallacher Memorial Library, which includes both published and unpublished material from the Communist Party of Great Britain, and much else besides. The 'Anon' songs were all typed on an italic font typewriter, a very unusual instrument. I wonder if they were ever sung in public? The tunes are an eclectic bunch, not from the Scots or American folk traditions, so the maker was not part of the Scottish folk scene. 'God Save The People' is from the stage musical *Godspell*.

'Let Him Go Let Him Tarry' and 'Has Anybody Here Seen Kelly' were popular tunes in the 1940s, and it is not clear what tune 'Liberty' is – there are a couple of unlikely candidates whose metres do not agree with the 'Under Heath' song. I can get no clues to a tune called 'Glory To The 17th Battalion'. More than one 17th Battalion featured in Britain's wars.

'God Save The Shipyards', 'United All' and 'The Freedom Song' are in standard English language that smacks of the Hymnal, as does 'Let Him Go Don't Let Him Tarry', though this and 'Has Anybody Here Seen Kelly?' use popular music hall tunes and lyric references. 'Kelly', 'U.C.S' and 'Under Heath There's

Nothing For Us' employ Scots-inflected language and touches of angry humour. 'The Freedom Song' works off James Connolly's uncompromising 'Rebel Song', a favourite of the bands that led 1930s Hunger Marches through Scotland into Edinburgh. Are the first three from one hand, the others from another maker, all typed up in the Communist Party offices, and perhaps sung at Party events but not carried to the public demos? Can any reader of this book retrieve their history for us?

As well as being sung, some lyrics were printed. When the editor of a Glasgow free press newspaper wanted lyrics to illustrate an article, I gave him Jim McLean's two songs, and for want of more I penned a few simplistic verses to the favourite Glesca tune of 'Ye Canny Shove Yer Grannie'. It began 'You can bet you'll aye see us at UCS, aifter Labour and the Tories have traded in their jauries'. I added a note to explain what type of marble was a jaurie.

In 1972, Jim McLean produced and issued on his Nevis record label a 'victory LP'. Danny Kyle's sleeve note said in part 'The artistes involved and Nevis Productions have given their services free to show solidarity with the new Clydesiders.' Jim McLean later explained how the LP came about: 'I was approached by Danny Kyle, an old friend, if I could do anything for the strike / work-in, and I went up to Glasgow and met Jimmy Airlie. I proposed making an LP which they (the committee) could buy for 50p and sell on, thereby making money for the strike fund. Myself and all concerned waived any profits. The 50p covered studio time, pressings and LP sleeves. I gathered the artists around and produced the album *Unity Creates Strength*. Jimmie Macgregor wrote 'Pack Your Tools and Go' specifically for the LP, but the other song, 'The Highland Medley' [sung by Hall and Macgregor] is just a traditional selection recorded and sung by many people before.'

The other tracks on the LP include McLean's two UCS songs sung by well-known multi-talented Alastair MacDonald, Kyle's 'Great Iron Ship' and another from him about a father playing with his child. Famed Scottish folksinger Alex Campbell sings two songs, one of them from the American tradition about coalminers, the other his own 'Been on the Road' about his travelling life. Hamish Henderson's trenchant 'John Maclean March', and the humorous 'SS Shieldhall' about the 'sludgy' boat that took Glasgow's human excrement down the Clyde to be dumped at sea, are performed by Arthur Johnstone and the Laggan. Irish songwriter Dominic Behan contributes his fierce 'Connolly Was There'. Only three of the songs in this volume are on the thirteen track LP, but the others included relate closely to the theme of unity and action. The second last track is by singer Ian Campbell. Several Ian Campbells have been active as songmakers or pipers during Scotland's Folk Song Revival. This Campbell was from Govan, played bass and, like many Glaswegians, he preferred to sing in a fairly convincing Southern American 'country music style' voice. His self-penned contribution titled 'Pass Round the Whisky' is a rather melancholy yet determined assertion of the human spirit which speaks of the 'great shipyards in the town I was born', and states 'You have made of me something I was not before'. The LP 'Finale', featuring all the performers, is a solidarity squib to the tune 'John Brown's Body' that says 'The shipyards in Clydeside had their back against the wall, then the workers took control. Glory, glory, we don't need you anymore, put the workers in control.'

After the struggle, the laments. To Tony McCarthy's early one were added elegiac others from **Iain Ingram, Leo Coyle** and **Geordie McIntyre**. Ingram's best known song, much sung in the Revival, is 'Annie McKelvie'. His song here is an eloquent funeral oration for the yards.

Leo Coyle penned enough songs of his native Clydebank and Scotland to fill a CD, *Clyde Born*, on which the performances are by his son and daughter. Coyle said re his shipyards song, 'Much has been written and sung in praise of the Clyde and the great ships built there, but little written or sung are about the hellish conditions endured by the workers who built them. Since I served my time in the shipyards, I lived with the unique humour and tenacity of the Clyde shipyard worker to overcome and survive in spite of so many betrayals.'

Geordie McIntyre is an influential Glasgow singer and folk club organizer who has done important work as a folk song collector. He is a prolific creator of fine songs. His 'Writing On the Wall' was made for a 1979 BBC Radio Scotland programme called *Requiem for the Clyde*. McIntyre comments on the song, 'In this age of globalisation and heartless "market forces" what price loyalty to the employer or vice versa?'

The editors have included one song that relates not to UCS but to the wider industrial struggle in Scotland. The tune is much older, best known as the song 'The Wark o the Weavers', which praised the handloom weavers of Forfar. **Dick Gaughan**'s recent song looking back to the 1984 Miners' Strike, 'Keep Looking at the Light', sombrely reminds the reader that joint action does not always win, yet urges us to 'keep working for the change'.

It is most appropriate that the final song is by **Arthur Johnstone**. A Glasgow left winger, powerfully voiced Johnstone sang for some years with The Laggan folk group, then as an unaccompanied solo singer. For many years he ran the Star Folk Club, which at the time met in the Communist Party's Glasgow HQ. One of the foremost singers at demos, when Johnstone heard that this book was mooted he was moved to write his own excellent tribute to the yard workers, and unlike the requiems of other songmakers, he ends on a positive note, pointing out the present-day result of what the work-in achieved. The past still lives.

The Great Iron Ship

Words and music by Danny Kyle; final chorus added during the UCS work-in

I'm working on deck of the great iron ship,
Hell below zero, slung over the side.
Riveters' guns play tattoos on the hull.
We're the men that build ships on the Clyde

> *With your hammering, your caulking,*
> *Your gouging and your burning,*
> *Snow in your face and tired inside,*
> *The conditions are bad, apprentice young fella.*
> *Don't hang around, get out with the tide.*

Look out down below, a hammer is falling!
Beware, live cables lie on the wet decks!
'No smoking on board', say your safety precautions;
And flames from the burners, they blister your neck.

> *Chorus*

Three men were sent down to the old double bottom.
To protect them, they wore safety hats on their heads.
But gas got ignited in that small cramped compartment.
One was dragged out, but the others lay dead.

> *Chorus*

A fur-coated lady swings a bottle of champagne,
And breaks it against the iron ship's side.
The workers stand cheering, their conditions forgotten;
With their caps in the air, it's their launching-day pride.

> *With your hammering, your caulking,*
> *Your gouging and your burning,*
> *Snow in your face and tired inside,*
> *The conditions are bad, apprentice young fella,*
> *But please hang around and fight from inside.*
> *Please hang around and fight from inside.*

Photograph by Alex Young

Pack Your Tools and Go

Words by Jimmie Macgregor; tune 'Drill Ye Tarriers, Drill',
traditional American song about mining

Monday morning early by the clock
The Clydeside men were working on the dock,
When the gaffer comes round, he says bad news,
The Upper Clyde is bound to close.

So pack your tools and go. Pack your tools and go.
For the word's been said, the yards are dead,
The big old gates are closing,
So pack your tools and go.

The word's gone round in London town,
The yards all round are closing down,
You're all on the dole, so no more booze,
And no more for the kids' new shoes.

So pack your tools and go. Pack your tools and go.
For it's just too bad, but you've all been had,
As your fathers were before you,
So pack your tools and go.

Along came a man whose name was Reid.
Says he, we'll win if we keep the heid,
For we've got the brains and the old know-how.
We won't bow down and we won't kow-tow.

Pick up your tools, let's go. Pick up your tools, let's go.
For we'll make our way without their say.
And keep the hammers ringing.
Pick up your tools, let's go.

Here's a word for the man down south.
You're big in the belly and big in the mouth.
You live far away and you don't give a damn
For the life and the pride of a working man.

So pack your tools and go. Pack your tools and go.
For we're here to say you've had your day,
It's time that you were leaving.
So pack your tools and go.

You're on the run, your day is done,
So pack your tools and go.

Wi' Jimmy Reid and Airlie

Words by Matt McGinn; tune 'Bonny Lassie I'll Lie Near Ye Yet', traditional Scottish song

> *Bonny lassie rise and dress yersel',*
> *The day we maun be early.*
> *We're marchin' in tae Glesga toon*
> *Wi' Jimmy Reid and Airlie.*

Put on the scarlet scarf I bought ye, hen,
For fourteen and a tanner,
Tae match the colours at oor heid,
Oor scarlet tartan banner.

> *Chorus*

Oor faithers fought this fight before -
Maclean, McShane fought fairly -
And we will fight them once again
Wi' Jimmy Reid and Airlie.

> *Chorus*

The Clydeside men are angry noo,
They're no' goin' on the dole queue.
Tell they men in London toon
We're takin' o'er control noo.

> *Bonny lassie rise and dress yersel',*
> *The day we maun be early.*
> *We're marchin' in tae Glesga toon*
> *Wi' Jimmy Reid and Airlie.*

Yes, Yes, U.C.S.

Words by Matt McGinn; tune 'Skip to my Lou', traditional American children's song

> *Tell 'em on the radio,*
> *Tell 'em on the press:*
> *I want my job and I want no less;*
> *No more dole day doldrums.*

Shipyard born and shipyard bred,
Shipyards till the day I'm dead.
I've got kids that must be fed;
Want no dole day doldrums.

> *Chorus*

A man came here from London town;
Half an hour, he looked around.
He said, 'Close that shipyard down';
Gave me dole day doldrums.

> *Chorus*

I've worked long, and I've worked hard,
Shivered in the cold in the old shipyard.
I do like butter and I don't like lard;
Want no dole day doldrums.

> *Tell 'em on the radio,*
> *Tell 'em on the press:*
> *I want my job and I want no less;*
> *No more dole day doldrums.*

Head Teeth

Words by Jim McLean; tune 'Casey Jones', traditional American song

The workers in the UCS were told they had to go,
But they began to organise and told the Tories, 'No!
It's you who'll be a-movin' cause you got us in this mess.
Now you're goin' to get the message from the UCS.'

>*Edward Heath,*
>*We have taken over.*
>*Edward Heath,*
>*We'll have nothing less.*
>*Edward Heath,*
>*We have got a work-in,*
>*And now you're gonna listen to the UCS.*

So Edward said to Davies, 'You go up and see the men.
I'm far too busy sailing, and I'm scared of Wedgwood Benn.'
So Davies came to Glasgow, but the boys were not impressed,
And Davies got a Harvey Smith from UCS.

>*Chorus*

When Davies got to London, someone said that Ted was lost,
So he took his little telescope and scanned the English coast,
And there upon the skyline, sailing far into the West,
Ted was going like the clappers from the UCS.

>*Edward Heath,*
>*We have taken over.*
>*Edward Heath,*
>*We'll have nothing less.*
>*Edward Heath,*
>*We have got a work-in,*
>*And now you're gonna listen to the UCS.*

A Shipyard on the Clyde

Words by Danny Couper; tune 'Hey Tutti Taitie', a traditional Scottish tune believed to have been played before Bruce at Bannockburn, later associated with 'Scots Wha Hae', written by Robert Burns

There's a shipyard on the Clyde where working men stood side by
side.
They took yon Tories and laid their pride for abody here tae see.
Yon Heath and Davies they did rue when they took on the
Clydeside crew,
And ah the boys did mak them spew, like the sickly things they be.

For they hae wakened the ghosts o men, the Gallachers, the John
Macleans.
They never thocht they'd rise again; well, just you watch and see!
For Jimmy Reid, Jim Airlie, too, and ah their stewards are but a few,
Tae keep the boys frae aff the brew, will fight wae dignity.

On Scotland's pound they're prood tae show the John Broon's yaird
sae fine and braw.
Ye canny tak that awa wae nothing left tae be,
For it was by the toil and sweat o caulkers, welders and their mates
That launched Queen Lizzie from their gates, their pride for years
tae be.

So we'll send this message loud and clear for ah yon faceless men tae
hear,
That the Clyde's oor heritage sae dear, and we will do or dee.
Aye, there's a shipyard on the Clyde where working men stood side
by side.
They took yon Tories and laid their pride for abody here tae see.

God Save the Shipyards

*Words anonymous; tune 'God Save The People', a song from the
1970 American musical, Godspell, by Schwartz and Tebelak*

When will you save the shipyards, O God of mercy, when?
Why must we be redundant, redundant once again?
We've played our part from day to day,
Yet work as naught, we're tossed away,
To face in want our prospects grey,
God save the shipyards.

We live in bondage ever, no time for mirth and song,
Our chains we long to sever, we wish to right this wrong,
Go, say the Tories, go and die,
We need you not, nor heed your sigh,
Come back when war clouds black the skies,
Then God will save the shipyards.

When will you save the shipyards, O God of mercy, when?
The shipyards, Lord, the shipyards,
Fill them once more with men,
God save the shipyards, ours they are,
Not just in war make them your care,
Give us them now, lift our despair,
God save the shipyards.

Has Anybody Here Seen Kelly?

Words anonymous; tune 'Kelly From The Isle Of Man', music hall song written by Murphy and Letters in 1908

Has anybody here seen Kelly, Kelly the shipyard man,
Has anybody here seen Kelly, nail him if you can,
He's the boy tae put the yairds full go,
Put an end tae the moans frae Heath and Co.
Has anyone here seen Kelly, Kelly the shipyard man,?

We'll ask Jimmy Reid and Airlie, if they've worked oot a plan.
We'll ask Jimmy Reid and Airlie, if everything's in han'.
They's the lads who'll no just tak' a No,
Tae get us work they'll strike a blow,
An fix up a deal wi' Kelly, Kelly the shipyard man.

'Like William Gallacher before them, McGahey and Reid spoke to their own class in their own language, the 'truth' of which was supported, indeed 'guaranteed' in part by the manner of its delivery: argumentative, colourful, humour-fuelled, well-read, intelligent, working class, autodidactic – as liable to burst into Burns' songs or quote Keats as to discourse on the trouble in Ireland, Ibrox or Celtic Park. These people wanted a modern progressive Scotland because they knew the present one was jiggered, regressive, held-back.'
Alistair Findlay

U.C.S.

Words anonymous; tune 'John Brown's Body', traditional American anti-slavery song

In every yaird alang the Clyde, the situation's grave,
The working lads entrenched inside they never shall enslave,
They fight for freedom every one, and just keep working on
And they just keep working on.

> *The Hell wi' Ridley, Heath and Davies,*
> *The Hell wi' Ridley, Heath and Davies,*
> *They say it is too late tae save us*
> *But we'll show them they're not on.*

We're working for our livelihood and for a brighter dawn,
We'll earn our bread by honest sweat, we want nae burroo or pawn,
And Heath and Co can dae their worse, we'll sune mak' them begaun
And jist keep working on.

> *Chorus*

The Thirties are behind us when oor faithers walked the streets,
Their shirts in rags, their troosers bags, worn buits upon their feet,
They didna hae a main tae spend tae gie their bairns a treat
And their hate lives on and on.

> *Chorus*

Trade Unionists support us, applaud oor fighting stand,
Donations they send pouring in from branches through the land,
They ken oor fight is theirs as weel, and we'll give nae remand,
We'll jist keep fighting on.

> *Chorus*

Oor birthright is the right tae work and earn oor daily bread,
We are na' slaves, we still are men who'll never bow the head,
We cairry on the fight begun by long since martyred dead,
And we'll ne'er be put upon.

> *The Hell wi' Ridley, Heath and Davies,*
> *The Hell wi' Ridley, Heath and Davies,*
> *They say it is too late tae save us*
> *But we'll show them they're not on.*

'...the UCS struggle reveals a potential of great practical importance today. It demonstrates, in embryo, that the organised working class does indeed have the unique ability to unite an alliance against monopoly rule and, in doing so, open the way to wider social transformation.'
John Foster and Charles Woolfson

'In 1971, I emigrated to Australia with my husband and two children... My brother William, who was only 20 at that time, had just completed his apprenticeship as a Shipwright in Connells, and had just got his papers. He decided to come with us because he couldn't see a future in the shipyards, and no call for his skills... My husband and William got work in Williamstown Dockyard in Melbourne. In those days there was no Internet and Sky News, so news of the UCS Work-In and events back home came through the Trade Union Movement... My husband Kenny and I returned to Clydebank in 1974. Kenny got a job in Yarrows... Clydebank and Australia were linked once again in 2000, when simultaneous marches for justice for Asbestos victims were held, organised through the CFMEU in Australia and Clydebank Community Unemployed Resource Centre (CCURC).'
Mary Collins

United All

Words anonymous; tune 'Glory To The 17th Battalion'

United all we stand firm on this issue,
Righteous anger makes us take this stand,
We refuse as one to be redundant,
At the behest of Heath's vile Tory band.
On the Clyde we work and act as brothers,
And our purpose we'll make clear,
This is our land and these our yards forever,
Must be swept of misery and fear.

Come fight, we all must fight, our cause is right there's no denying,
Come fight with all your might, put them to flight, our banners flying,
Come fight and end this night as one together we'll advance,
With our blood we'll guard our river bank and the Red Clyde's name
                                                            enhance.

We shall make the yards ring with our hammers,
Build fine ships to send to every land,
Show the Tories what the Scots are made of,
Give no quarter or remand.
In Glasgow we are mates together,
We shall never yield, tis clear,
With our blood we will, if needs be,
Put an end to misery and fear.

Come fight, we all must fight, our cause is right there's no denying,
Come fight with all your might, put them to flight, our banners flying,
Come fight and end this night as one together we'll advance,
With our blood we'll guard our river bank and the Red Clyde's name
                                                            enhance.

The Freedom Song

Words anonymous; tune 'A Rebel Song', by G.W. Crawford, associated with words by James Connolly, who was shot in 1916 after the Irish Easter Rising

Come brothers join the mighty throng that guards the shipyard gate,
Our work it must go on and on, we must defeat the great,
The great who seek to kill our town, to leave it cold and dead,
Who hear no plea, nor children's sob, and steal our very bread.

We'll cut the binding thong that stifles freedom's song,
The song to end all tyranny and free us from our fears,
Then exploitation done, we will live free in the sun,
Banish workless night and see at last, through eyes now clear of tears.

Nothing in our hearts impaling, as workers' dawn appears,
Gone! Gone! The ropes that bound us, no more hear tyrants' jeers,
Our banner high above us flying plain to see,
With strength of will and unity at last we shall be free.

Then long in Labour history shall live the glorious name,
Of all who fight reaction, beat Tories at their game,
Then ever more will Clyde-built ships sail proudly on the sea,
And we again to Tory lords, shall never bend the knee.

Let Him Go, Don't Let Him Tarry

Words anonymous; tune 'Let Him Go Let Him Tarry', traditional Irish song

Let him go, don't let him tarry, let him sink and fail to swim,
Heath never cared for us and we don't care for him,
Let him in the ocean founder, it will bring to us great joy,
And we'll soon replace him with a left wing Labour boy.

Let him go and join old Harry, while we sing a parting hymn,
For while he is at the top our working prospects dim.
We shall give a sailor's farewell, while he sinks into the deep,
Then toddle home contented to have a peaceful sleep.

'Arriving back from my time as a music student, into the Glasgow of July, 1971, I was swept up in the activity around the work-in, leafleting, selling The Worker, etc. I found the solidarity concerts – at Clydebank Town Hall (September 22, 1971), Woodside Hall (November 14, 1971), Green's Playhouse (April 30, 1972), etc., very inspiring. But I made my own contribution in the way I knew best – composing music – and wrote 'Resistance – Music for Saxophones' dedicated to the success of the work-in. The London Saxophone Quartet performed an extract of it on STV in early December, 1971. (Only recently did it receive a full performance from Sax Ecosse!) I was pleased to have been able to present a copy to Jimmy Reid when I met him at Glasgow University – he had been elected Rector – on December 13, 1971. So as well as from folk musicians, support came from classical players and composers such as Bill Sweeney and the great clarinet teacher, performer and conductor, Alan Hacker, who led his Royal Academy of Music students in a solidarity concert in St Pancras Town Hall, London and at The Roundhouse in January, 1972. Forty years on, I aim to compose another piece – for brass, saxophones, Arthur Johnstone and The Whistlebinkies – to celebrate and bring back that spirit of resistance.'
Eddie McGuire

Photograph by Alex Young

Under Heath There's Nothing for Us

Words anonymous; tune 'Liberty'

Under Heath there's nothing for us, misery alone he'll bring,
Show your hate and sing this chorus, through the rafters let it ring.

> *The hell wi' Heath and a' his cronies, founder him and a' his crew,*
> *A' his facts are just baloney, lies that mak' the workers spew.*

Let him go and play his organ, lead his choir in songs of praise,
Whilst wi' us he acts the gorgon, deprive us of our food and claithes.

> *Chorus*

See the dole queue there before us, want and fear on every face,
And nae matter whit a man does, he just canna get a place.

> *Chorus*

Day by day the workless total spirals up, unending it would seem,
Not jist here, the symptoms they are global, wherever Capital reigns
supreme.

> *The hell wi' Heath and a' his cronies, founder him and a' his crew,*
> *A' his facts are just baloney, lies that mak' the workers spew.*

The Final Ship

words and music: Iain Ingram

(CHORUS)

Tae the auld yairds lang forgotten O'er the cobbled stanes weel trodden, There is nowt tae see o' whit used tae be. It's a' pulled doon and broken.

(VERSE 1)

Thro' the rusty gates I'm staring At the place we a' stood swearing. When the final ship went doon the slip, We knew the end was nearing

The Final Ship

Words and music by Iain Ingram

> *Tae the auld yairds lang forgotten*
> *O'er the cobbled stanes weel trodden,*
> *There is nowt tae see o' whit used tae be.*
> *It's a' pulled doon and broken.*

Thro' the rusty gates I'm staring
> At the place we a' stood swearing.
When the final ship went doon the slip,
> We knew the end was nearing.

> *Chorus*

But the worst was never knowing
> Wha was next in line for going,
And I saw my peers reduced to tears,
> Their pride and status blown.

> *Chorus*

'Twas a Clydeside institution
> They had nae mair for using.
It was in the news how oor toon wid lose
> Her jobs and fine tradition.

> *Chorus*

Noo ye'll never see much finer
> Than a Clyde-built Cunard liner.
While she sails wi' grace ower the ocean waves,
> It's her makers I'll remember.

> *Tae the auld yairds lang forgotten*
> *O'er the cobbled stanes weel trodden,*
> *There is nowt tae see o' whit used tae be.*
> *It's a' pulled doon and broken.*

Writing on the Wall

Words by Geordie McIntyre; tune 'John Anderson My Jo John'

'The writing's on the wall, me lads,'
We heard auld Willie say.
'It's time tae leave your sinkin' ships
An' just cry it a day.
The Clyde it's a back number noo,
It isnae worth a damn!
They're turnin' docksides intae parks.
So, get out, while ye's can.'

Auld Willie, he's just fifty-one,
An' it's a cryin' shame.
He did his bit on mony a ship.
Aye, a man that knew the game.
He worked the yards as boy and man,
In rain and sleet and snow.
Then came the final bonus,
He was told he had tae go!

That wis just a year ago,
An' Willie's still on the dole.
For a' yon hard endeavour
It's a gey hard thing tae thole.
So we'll stay and fight for the right tae work,
For Willie, and a' the rest.
For it's no just shipyard workers
That they're puttin' tae the test.

Song o the Yard

Words by Leo Coyle; tune 'The Laird of Cockpen', a traditional Scottish song

Through the eyes o a young man born on the Clyde,
When the pulse o humanity turned on the tide,
An a nation that depended on ships for its trade,
Turned a blind eye on the price that was paid.

Raw cauld is the mist on the river at dawn,
Wi coat collars up, the men hurry on;
The keel maun be laid ere a new ship is born,
An yae might lose a shift if yer late for the horn.

The frames o the hull in the cauld mist are lost,
A skeleton dressed in a mantle o frost,
A spectre sae drear t'would daunt even the brave,
For there's nae caulder place tween the womb an the grave.

Wi the reek o steel burnin an the clangin o plates,
The chokin on fumes an shoutin o mates,
Wi the din o the caulkers vibratin the shell,
A ship on the stocks is just organised hell.

But there's aye caustic humour an witty retort,
An endless comment aboot wimen an sport,
For it's wimen an horses an who scored the goal,
That sustain men in life such conditions tae thole.

On Kilbowie Hill the beeches stand tall,
Oer men frae the yard who hae given their all,
One moment alive and the next just a wreck,
Covered oer wi coats on a cauld rusty deck.

They were aye in the news when the critics cried oot,
Just countin up hours that's lost in dispute,
An I wonder, did they earn their livin as hard
As the men that were building the ships in the yard?

Noo, there must be oer many who think we were daft,
Takin pride in oor labour, oor skill an oor craft,
Buildin luxury liners, empresses and queens,
That ever tae sail on was far yond oor dreams.

Through the eyes o an auld man, I gaze on the river,
An the young jobless men, wonderin if it's forever,
Wi Scotland united, we'll still turn the tide,
An return to its glory, the Valley o Clyde.

'The UCS was inspirational for myself and many of my generation. The
workers' courage and determination, international solidarity, and the magical
oratory of Jimmy Reid aroused the 'latent seeds' of political and social justice,
which became a way of life.'
Danny McCafferty

'If you were alive in 1972, 73, 74, you would have thought this was a great
victory for the workers, which it was, and then what happened? First of all,
Thatcherism rolled back the support of the state for Scottish industry in the
1980s. Second, the wider sense of support for Scottish rights seemed to
disintegrate in 1979 with the failed referendum, and finally... there was the
virtual annihilation of Clyde shipbuilding. By the time you got into the early
1990s, the River Clyde was virtually silent... Unfortunately, the historical forces
at work in the last quarter of the 20th Century were against the kind of values
and standpoint that Jimmy Reid and others stood for.'
Tom Devine

The Death of the Clyde

Words and music by Tony McCarthy

> *The big ships are gone, the boatyards stand idle,*
> *And they must leave Glasgow, no more may they bide.*
> *Their torches are dimmed and their hammers are silent,*
> *And the cranes stand still, mourners at the death of the Clyde.*

Their fathers once farmed on a croft in the islands,
Their fathers bred kine on the banks and the braes;
Their fathers were kings with the clans in the Highlands,
But like the flowers of the forest are all gone away.

> *Chorus*

They then came to Clydebank, took the streets of the city
For the call of the curlew, the whip of the wind;
Worked days of darkness and nights without pity,
With memories of moorlands that they'd left behind.

> *Chorus*

And when the Red Flag flew over their homeland
And big John Maclean came home to the Clyde,
They dreamed that at last they might live in their own land,
Working with dignity, resting with pride.

> *Chorus*

But now it's farewell to the nation that bore them,
To London, America, Hamburg they'll go.
There's no hope for Scotland, and no living for them;
First we cleared out the Highlands, now the cities also.

> *The big ships are gone, the boatyards stand idle,*
> *And they must leave Glasgow, no more may they bide.*
> *Their torches are dimmed and their hammers are silent,*
> *And the cranes stand still, mourners at the death of the Clyde.*

Keep Looking At The Light

Words and music Dick Gaughan
© 2011 Dick Gaughan - all rights reserved
Published by PRS for music

The year I best re - mem - ber it was nine-teen eigh-ty

four When the bru-tal fist of ty-ran-ny came pound-ing down the

door And the tears of ang-ry wom-en and the grief of des-perate

men cut a sav-age wound deep in my soul that 'll nev-er heal a-gain And

in that time of strgg - le, through the sor-row and the pain a

small voice some-where in the dark be - gan to gent-ly sing

Keep look-ing at the light keep your eyes on the road a-head

keep on work-ing for the change that has to come Keep look-ing at the

light When those with no-thing left to lose de - fied the migh-ty

State and stood with pride and dig-ni-ty out - side the coll-iery gates My

sis-ters and my broth-ers were fight-ing for their lives but

more than that they fought so that some de-cen-cy'd sur - vive

Keep Looking at the Light

Words and tune by Dick Gaughan

The year I best remember
It was 1984
When the brutal fist of tyranny
Came pounding down the door,
And the tears of angry women
And the grief of desperate men
Cut a savage wound deep in my soul
That'll never heal again.
And in that time of struggle,
Through the sorrow and the pain,
A small voice somewhere in the dark
Began to gently sing:

> *Keep looking at the light.*
> *Keep your eyes on the road ahead.*
> *Keep on working for the change that has to come.*
> *Keep looking at the light.*

When those with nothing left to lose
Defied the mighty State,
And stood with pride and dignity
Outside the colliery gates,
My sisters and my brothers
Were fighting for their lives,
But more than that, they fought
So that some decency'd survive.

You can call me a romantic,
Call me what you will,
But the flame I saw those troubled times
Is burning brightly still.
What the cynics could not understand
Is what they could not kill:
The power of human dignity,
The strength of human will.

And as one year comes to ending
And another year begins,
I clearly hear the words that small voice
Taught me how to sing:

> *Keep looking at the light.*
> *Keep your eyes on the road ahead.*
> *Keep on working for the change that has to come.*
> *Keep looking at the light.*

'With scabrous song, Scotland is surely among the Top Ten. The Makars, Burns, MacDiarmid, are all there, and in the last fifty years there has been a resurgence of this genre... If we are heading in Lillian Hellman's memorable phrase 'to Scoundrel Time', the wielders of the scabrous will come singing to our aid, and we should welcome them and join in, and thereby help continue a truly great tradition.'
Janey Buchan

'Much of the success of the workforce in building and maintaining unity and creating an extraordinarily broad alliance at home and abroad was down to the leadership of the struggle and the creative tactics and language which it used. The idea of a work-in, rather than a strike, symbolised the positive emphasis on the Scottish work ethic. This transformed the battle from just another industrial dispute into an epic struggle for a basic human right – the right to work... Oh how we need victories like that today!'
Alan Mackinnon

Doon through the Years

Words by Arthur Johnstone; tune traditional Scottish or Irish.
Several lyrics have been written for it, particularly 'Nicky Tams',
an early 20th Century song of North-East farm work, by G.S.
Morris, who claimed to have composed the tune.

I've worked for over forty years
Frae Fairfields doon tae Broons.
I've even worked at the Tail o' the Bank,
Wi the lads frae Greenock Toon.
I've been on trials on the measured mile,
Noo I've done it aa wi pride,
For I've helped tae build the giant ships
That sail the oceans wide.

When we built the new Q4,
It was a mighty sight.
There was electricians, engineers,
And even the odd shipwright.
There was Harry the Horse who selt us tools,
The best American brand.
He said he got them frae New York,
But his story didnae stand.

I was workin back in Fairfields
When the word was passed aroon:
The government was shuttin doon
Aa the yairds in Glesga Toon.
They said oor yairds they didnae pay
And we would have tae go.
But the men aa stood together,
And we proudly answered No.

Jimmy Reid and Airlie,
Barr, Gilmour, and the rest,
They aa went doon tae London Toon
The government tae face.
They telt them we were workin in,

That we were gaun tae stay.
When the government relented,
UCS had won the day.

As I look back doon through the years
At the changes we have seen,
They're buildin aa they yuppie flats
Aa the way tae Glesga Green.
But the Govan lads are workin on
And Yarrows seems alright.
I hate tae think whit might have been
If we hidnae put up that fight.

Notes on the Poems and Poets

David Betteridge

One approach to appreciating our selection of poems is to take them in chronological sequence: not in order of their dates of composition, but according to when in a storyline of events each one fits. That is how we have sequenced the poems here, starting with **Freddy Anderson**'s vigorous piece of historical scene-setting, 'Ballad of the Red Clyde'.

Thanks are due to the poet's son, Paul, for giving permission to us to publish the ballad here. He was careful to point out that his father, a staunchly principled man, would have had misgivings regarding some of the poems and songs by other authors that appear here, namely those that contain praise for his former friend, Jimmy Reid. The poet strongly disapproved of the latter's public criticism of the leadership of the Miners' Strike in 1984, though not, it has to be said, of the strike itself. This criticism the poet saw as unhelpful and divisive, giving comfort to the miners' enemies. Many on the Left agreed, and still agree. None of this alters the fact that 'Ballad of the Red Clyde' deserves a place in these pages. Never mind the company in which it finds itself, in this broad kirk of a collection! It enhances the other poems by its presence. Freddy Anderson, originally from County Monaghan, was a member of the Clyde Group of left wing and republican poets that Hamish Henderson, for one, so admired. Other members included John Kincaid, George Todd, and Thurso Berwick, the last being the alias of Morris Blythman, well known as a folk singer, songmaker, and teacher. (One of his pupils was Ewan McVicar, whose Notes on our selection of songs appear elsewhere in the book.) Freddy Anderson wrote, not only a mountain of memorable poems and songs, but plays as well, including one about his admired John Maclean, *Krassivy* (performed at the Edinburgh Festival, 1979), and a satirical novel about the misadventures of a 'wise fool', *Oiney Hoy* (published in 1989).

'Ballad of the Red Clyde' employs the imagined voice of the river to tell, in part, a similar tale to that given in Ken Currie's

History Paintings, held in the People's Palace on Glasgow Green. See also John Couzin's *Radical Glasgow*, available on Glasgow Caledonian University's website. In presenting a people's view of history, the ballad combats 'fake historians' and 'hiders of the truth', thus endorsing our book's motto text, by John Berger, about not letting our past suffer 'erasure'. It sets the scene for the UCS-related poems in our selection.

Just as the work-in excited, and still excites, a complex range of emotions, depending on one's viewpoint, so does the very business of building ships. In **Bill Sutherland**'s three poems included here from his 1989 collection, *A Clydeside Lad*, we encounter such a range, strongly expressed, and strongly compressed, sometimes within the space of a few lines. 'Whit god's, whit divvil's beast is this?' he wonders as he contemplates 'the beauty o a liner' under construction, 'a black Leviathin... Fed fat wae the sweat o workers'. He explores the fear of a first-day apprentice, wishes for a saving 'iron grace', and then notes the humour of 'the gruff big men'. And, in his account of the launching of a ship, he describes the 'powerfa love' and almost painful pride that the workers felt as they 'watched whit oor hauns hid built, oor ain' as it entered the water, 'a beauty oot a Hell'.

This same pride crops up again and again in our selection of songs and poems. It has a long tradition in the culture of Clydeside, being rooted in the belief that:

> *The Clyde is the greatest shipbuilding river the world has ever seen. The end of shipbuilding on the river will be a tragedy beyond the economic...*

So wrote Jimmy Reid in a column he contributed to *The Herald*, reprinted at the time of his death. Describing the upset of a group of workers when they heard that the *Queen Elizabeth* had been damaged by fire, and had capsized and sunk in Hong Kong harbour, he went on to observe that the ship 'might have belonged to Cunard, but these men knew it was their ship in a way that no legal title deeds could usurp.' The tradition of pride was an important element in the moral hegemony that the UCS work-in achieved. Without it, the months of struggle would have been even harder to sustain.

Bill Sutherland (1950-2005) was born and brought up in Dumbarton. He worked as a primary school teacher in Dalmuir, and worked later at the Denny Experimental Tank in Dumbarton. He was a member of the Dumbarton Writers' Group, where Chris Small, then the Literary Editor of *The Herald*, got to know him, and to admire his work. In the Introduction that he wrote for *A Clydeside Lad*, Chris Small wrote that, 'Bill Sutherland's collection of poems belongs firmly to a place, a speech, a community and a way of thinking and living...' Further: 'The scope is wider than a single view. It extends, with imaginative empathy, into other minds, and it moves backward and forward over more than one generation.' In doing so, and with such a strong musicality of language, the three poems that we have included serve to set the social and cultural scene for the poems that follow, in much the same way that Freddy Anderson's 'Ballad of the Red Clyde' sets the historical and political scene.

Thanks are due to Lizzie MacGregor at the Scottish Poetry Library for bringing Bill Sutherland's work to the editor's attention; to the editor of Clydeside Press, who first published *A Clydeside Lad*, and the staff at Dumbarton Public Library, for their combined help in putting the editor in contact with the poet's family; and to Catherine Sutherland, the poet's widow, for giving her permission for her husband's work to appear here. *A Clydeside Lad* cries out to be re-published, in an expanded edition.

'Struggle', by **Jim Aitken**, focuses on an important aspect of the work-in, namely the 'mental fight', to quote William Blake, that preceded and accompanied the practical business of steering the work-in to victory. The poem captures the spirit in which the debates were conducted, and the options considered. For background detail, readers may consult John Foster's and Charles Woolfson's *The Politics of the UCS Work-in*; or, for a dramatic presentation, Frank Miller's *Work-in*. Jim Aitken is a teacher of English in an Edinburgh secondary school. His publications include *Glory* (2001), and *Neptune's Staff and Other Formations* (2007). A play of his, *From Haddington to Palestine*, was performed at the Edinburgh Fringe in 2006. He is a member of Scottish PEN.

Photograph by Owen McGuigan

'Clearances: a Diptych', also by Jim Aitken, conjures up two pictures, both featuring a monumental statue, both suggesting a personal and political story. The first poem, 'Redemption', commemorates the Highland Clearances. The second, 'Clyde-built', written specially for this book, addresses the long decline of heavy industry in the Central Belt. The parallels between the two histories include 'refusing to go down on the knee', a reference to La Pasionara's famous rallying cry from the time of the Spanish Civil War. Arthur Dooley's sculptural tribute to La Pasionara (Dolores Ibarruri) is located beside the Clyde, at Customs House Quay, Glasgow. The other statue mentioned by the poet is The Emigrants Statue in Helmsdale, by Gerald Laing. Its design, a family group, suggests both grief (at a people's forced departure from their homeland) and hope (regarding future achievements in new homes around the world).

Tessa Ransford's 'Counting' reminds us of the sort of economic calculation that informed the government's thinking in 1971-72, as before, and since: the sort of calculation in which money 'counts', and the majority of people do not. A similar critique informed Jimmy Reid's rectorial address, *Alienation*, delivered at the height of the work-in, when Reid was installed as the students' elected Rector of Glasgow University (April, 1972). 'Profit,' he said, 'is the sole criterion used by the establishment to evaluate economic activity. From the rat race to lame ducks. The vocabulary in vogue is a give-away. It is more reminiscent of a human menagerie than human society.'

Tessa Ransford's life's work in poetry, through poetry, celebrates a very different way of regarding the world, as in her 'Incantation 2000'. This millennium poem ends:

Who among us now will work
for light that penetrates the dark
for freedom climbing like the lark
for the democratic spark –
whose the tread that fits this mark?

She has published sixteen books of poems, starting with *Poetry of Persons* (1976) and culminating in a recent 'New and Selected Poems' volume, *Not Just Moonshine* (2008). She is a member of Scottish PEN, and was its President from 2003 to 2006. She was instrumental in establishing the Scottish Poetry Library, and the annual Callum Macdonald Memorial Prize for poetry pamphlets.

Edwin Morgan's poem about the work-in is the fifth of ten 'Glasgow Sonnets' that conclude his volume *From Glasgow to Saturn* (1973). The voice in the poem is a negative one. 'We have preferred silent slipways to the riveters' wit.' Whose voice is it? we wonder. It captures in condensed form – in the fourteen lines of a Petrarchan sonnet, in fact – some of the forces against which the work-in contended.

Edwin Morgan was Glasgow's first Poet Laureate, and Scotland's first Scots Makar. The very titles of many of his published works give a strong suggestion of their protean content and style. For instance: *The Second Life* (1968), *Instamatic Poems* (1972), *Wi the Haill Voice* (1972), *From Glasgow to Saturn* (1973), *Star-Gate* (1979), *From the Video Box* (1986), *Themes on a Variation* (1988), *Nothing Not Giving Messages* (1990), *Crossing the Border* (1990), *Hold Hands Among the Atoms* (1991), *Sweeping Out the Dark* (1994) and *A Book of Lives* (2007).

A trail-blazer in his practice of poetry, Edwin Morgan was also influential as a teacher and critic. An insight of his regarding Hamish Henderson's *Elegies for the Dead in Cyrenaica* (1948) is worth quoting here, as it applies with equal relevance to the several poems and songs in this book that are also elegiac: 'Henderson sees how his duty as an elegist must include more than remembrance... The dead will hold us in contempt if we fail to change society... ('The Sea, the Desert, the City', in *The Year Book of English Studies*, Volume 17, 1987).

Aonghas MacNeacail is a poet, songmaker, librettist, broadcaster, and tutor, who regularly represents Scotland, and Gaelic literature in particular, at overseas festivals and conferences. He writes in Gaelic, English and Scots.

His published volumes of poetry include *imaginary wounds* (1980), *an seachnadh / the avoiding* (1986), *rock and water* (1990), *oideachadh ceart / a proper schooling* (1997), and *laoidh an donais òig / hymn to a young demon* (2007). He was a consulting editor to *Leabhar Mar na Gaidhlig / The Great Book of Gaelic* (2002). As librettist, he collaborated with the composer William Sweeney on a chamber opera, *An Turus* (1998), based on the Diarmid and Grainne legend. The musicality of his language has attracted more than a dozen composers to set his words, including Ronald Stevenson (*neulag air fàire / small cloud on the horizon*), Alasdair Nicolson (an opera, *Sgathach / The Warrior Queen*), Donald Shaw (*Breisleach / Delirium* and other songs), Andy Thorburn (choral suite, *Tuath gu Deas*), and others. Written specially for this book, 'an còmhlachd / in unison' is an evocation of the UCS work-in, tapping into the poet's memory of the time, and fusing, in his own words, ' the tonalities, and to some extent the rhythms, of traditional Gaelic song' with a contemporary political awareness. Fearchar I. MacIllFhinnein (broadcaster) and Iseabail T. NicDhòmhnaill (journalist and folklorist) sum up the poem's achievement as follows: 'The poem's strong rhythms are reminiscent of the clatter of a shipyard. The metaphors make links with workers' movements, immovable geographic features and the river which sustains shipbuilding. The poem concludes with workers' pride in their ships and their readiness to work productively, in contrast to those who would create a "desert".'

'Banner and Roses' was written by **David Betteridge** during his editorial work on this book. Readers may like to reflect on the fact that John Lennon's famous utopian song 'Imagine', alluded to in the poem, was recorded in June and July, 1971, and released in September. His gift of roses and money to the work-in, jointly with Yoko Ono, also alluded to, was made between these events, in August. What influences were at work? we may wonder. What connections? The card that accompanied the roses bore the message 'Power to the People'. The editor is grateful to Pat Milligan for letting words of hers appear as a motto text for the poem. They are taken from a tape recorded contribution that she made to a Witness

Seminar on the UCS work-in, convened at Glasgow Caledonian University in May, 2002. These 30th anniversary witness statements constitute a valuable archive for historians and political activists alike.

Gerda Stevenson's 'I Am the *Esperance*' builds on the keel of an extended metaphor, that of an imagined fleet of ships returning to their place of origin, the Clyde. Each ship makes the voyage from a different part of the world's oceans, to show solidarity with the workers, whose yards are in danger of closure. Thus the poem gives expressive form to a key feature of the work-in that the shop stewards' *Bulletins* reported from the start, in a section called 'Finance and Solidarity'. In the first issue (1 September, 1971), for example, we read:

The messages of solidarity and financial support are continuing to pour in. This week's post contained £314 from Rolls Royce (Hillington), £1,000 from Chrysler, who hope to make it a weekly donation, and £1,00 from Dumbarton County Council. Three Soviet shipyards sent between them £2,700, and guilders from Amsterdam were converted to £554... Among the messages of solidarity were ones from Bergen in Norway and the Royal Shakespeare Company.

Gerda Stevenson is an actor/playwright, theatre director, and poet. Her extensive writing for radio includes dramatisations of classic Scottish novels – Mary Brunton's *Self-control* (2003), Nancy Brysson Morrison's *The Gowk Storm* (2005), Walter Scott's *The Heart of Midlothian* (2008, and Lewis Grassic Gibbon's *Sunset Song* (2009) – as well as her own plays: *The Apple Tree* (BBC Radio 4, 2011), and *Secrets,* a two-part drama about prostitution (BBC Radio Scotland, 2011). Her play *Federer Versus Murray* was shortlisted for the 2010 London Fringe Theatre Writing Award. Her short stories and poetry have appeared in magazines, newspapers, anthologies and literary journals throughout Britain and abroad. 'I Am the *Esperance*' was written specially for this book.

Brian Whittingham's two poems present contrasting views of the shipyards, one comic, the other elegiac. The first, 'At the

UCS Work-in', describes a canteen entertainment during the work-in, an act entailing the stretching of heavy-duty elastic as well as the audience's belief. The poem ends by mentioning the famous gift of roses sent to the work-in by John Lennon and Yoko Ono. The second poem, 'The Titan Crane', describes the crane that dominated John Brown's yard, birthplace of many famous ships. Now, however, the crane serves as a tourist attraction, in a ship-free setting. The poem could well be sub-titled 'Ghosts', as that is what a group of four ex-shipyard workers see in their mind's eye when they return to the 'barren panorama' with their wives.

Brian Whittingham started his working life as an apprentice in John Brown's. The *Q4* (Hull Number 736), later and better known as the *QE2*, was one of the ships he worked on. Now a poet, dramatist, short-story writer, photographer, and creative writing tutor, he has written about the yards e.g. in *Industrial Deafness* (1990) and in *Bowlers n Bunnets* (2009). He contributed to BBC Radio 2's radio ballad, *Ballad of the Big Ships* (2006), in which song and speech combine wonderfully after the fashion of the original series of radio ballads (1958-64), pioneered by Charles Parker, Ewan MacColl and Peggy Seeger. *Ballad of the Big Ships* features songs by John Tams e.g. 'Hold Back the Tide', and Karine Polwart e.g. 'You Can't Weld a Body (When It's Broken)'.

At the age of nineteen. **Donna Franceschild** was a shop steward for the American Federation of State, County and Municipal Employees in a large cafeteria in California. She led a successful occupation of a Board of Control meeting to demand the reinstatement of a fellow worker, and was also involved in an action in support of the nascent United Farmworkers Union. Since coming to Britain in the mid-Seventies, she has written extensively for stage, radio and television, engaging issues that have reflected her political and social commitment. A passionate mental health activist, she is best known for her BAFTA-winning drama serial, *Taking Over the Asylum* (1994). With the encouragement and critical support of Gerda Stevenson, she has recently begun to write poetry.

'Something Like Grief', written specially for this book, draws on an interview that Donna Franceschild conducted with a shipyard worker in 2000, during research for her BBC TV serial, *The Key* (shown in 2003). This drama follows the lives of three generations of women through the social history of the 20th Century. The poem has, in miniature, a similar range; and it operates from a similar woman's point of view, that of the grown-up daughter of a shipyard worker. On the day of the father's funeral, during the UCS work-in, the woman stands outside a pub, where she can hear the singing of some shipyard workers inside. It evokes in her a childhood memory of a much yearned-for bicycle that her father had promised to buy for her birthday, until a fellow worker of his was killed in the yard, and all the money for it went to the whip-round for the man's widow. The poem conveys this situation, reported to the author by the interviewee, and conveys also the principle of workers' solidarity, crucial to the success of the work-in, all in brilliantly realised dramatic detail.

The first part of **Alistair Findlay**'s 'Clydebuilt: the UCS' presents a picture of the work-in that is bristling with energy, all in one full-breathed sentence. The second part of the poem takes up the notion of 'arguing', the note on which the first part ended. It pursues it to a specific time and place, where a specific argument rages. Does the work-in represent a forward step in the class struggle, or a backward step? Is it an opportunity seized, or an opportunity lost? A work-in that keeps existing relations of production at UCS largely intact cannot be good... Such, or something similar, is the contention at the heart of the poet's adversary's case, a case that is still cogently argued by some on the Left. The poet's hostility to his adversary, named in the poem as Derek Hatton (later deputy leader of Liverpool City Council), as well as to a future Labour prime minister (also named) comes across with strong dramatic force, deliciously *ad hominem*.

In 'The Industrial Relations Act, 1971', Alistair Findlay shows us one of the sequels to the UCS work-in, namely the Conservative government's fight-back in the form of anti-union legislation. Being set in 1972, the poem is affirmative.

(The legislation was repealed in 1974, by the incoming Labour government.) The poet, formerly a footballer, latterly a social worker, has written and edited books about the beautiful game e.g. *100 Favourite Scottish Football Poems* (2007), or *Sex, Death and Football* (2003); and also books about 'the frontline of a fractured society' e.g. *Dancing with Big Eunice* (2010). See also *Shale Voices* (1999), and *The Love Songs of John Knox* (2006).

In the great sweep of his historical narrative, *A Dream of John Ball*, William Morris shows the leader of the Peasants' Revolt, John Ball, surveying future struggles according to the analysis of a later thinker-cum-activist, that is to say through the eyes of a character very like William Morris. (Such privilege of prophecy is denied us in the real world, regrettably.) Morris's alter ego concludes his reflections on the course of history with these often quoted words: 'I pondered how men fight and lose the battle, and the thing that they fought for comes about in spite of their defeat...' Looking back on the events of 1971-72, knowing what we now know, we might well modify these words, and the words that follow, and say: *We have pondered how people fight and win the battle, and the thing that they fought for fails to come about in spite of their victory, and when it comes turns out not to be what they meant, and other people have to fight for what they meant under another name.*

This 'pondering' is one of the strands of thought informing **David Betteridge**'s, 'Showing a Way'. It was written specially for this book, as was his 'Jaggily'. This latter poem owes its inspiration to a drawing of twining bramble shoots sent to him by **Bob Starrett**, formerly a painter at Yarrow's, currently employed part-time in the film industry. The cartoons that Starrett drew at the time, commenting on the work-in, appear elsewhere in this book. Other cartoons of his, serving a variety of causes, regularly appeared on posters and leaflets, mainly in his native Glasgow, over many years. They are collected in *Rattling the Cage* (1983). One of these cartoons, 'Nearly Time', showing Hitler waiting in the wings of the theatre of history, is a favourite of John Berger's, whose writings have greatly influenced both editor and cartoonist.

Chrys Salt has performed her poetry country wide, in France, and the USA. She is published in a wide variety of journals, magazines and anthologies, and broadcast on both Radios 3 and 4. Her collections include *Inside Out* (1989), *Daffodils at Christmas* (1998), *Greedy for Mulberries* (2008), and *Old Times* (2010). As well as poetry, she also writes theatre and radio plays, features and documentaries. She has been the recipient of several bursaries, grants and awards, including a National Media Award for her book *Here We Go: Women's Memories of the 1984/85 Miners' Strike*. This work of oral history derives its title from the song, included in that book, which was widely heard at the time of the strike. The words 'Here we go!' serve as a refrain:

> *We are women, we are strong,*
> *We are fighting for our lives*
> *Side by side with our men*
> *Who work the nation's mines,*
> *United by the struggle,*
> *United by the past,*
> *And it's – Here we go! Here we go!*
> *For the women of the working class.*

Chrys Salt divides her time between London and Galloway, where, in Gatehouse-of-Fleet, she is engaged in running The Bakehouse arts venue. She is also, with John Hudson, engaged in editing the literary magazine, *Markings*. 'He Wouldn't Want an Elegy' was written specially for this book. It makes a vigorous call for a vigorous kind of engaged poetry.

'Fresh Chapters', by **Danny McCafferty**, lives up to the optimism implicit in its title. Clydebank's Titan Crane, standing proud in a landscape of an 'Industry gone', is seen as a symbol, not only of the past, but of 'fresh chapters' waiting to be written. In this, the poem resembles Matt McGinn's great song, 'Ballad of the *Q4*', where we hear a rising generation assert to its elders that 'the Clyde is a river that'll no stand still, / You did gey well, but we'll do more.' The 'ghost ships' in 'Fresh Chapters' are of the future, unlike the ships imagined in Brian Whittingham's poem about the same landmark, 'The

Titan Crane'. The two poems complement one another beautifully. Danny McCafferty was formerly leader of West Dunbartonshire Council. He is currently chairperson of Clydebank Independent Resource Centre, an anti-poverty organisation. 'Fresh Chapters' is previously unpublished.

We started our sequence of poems with Freddy Anderson's long view of history, 'Ballad of the Red Clyde', given in the voice of the river. In it, we are brought from the 18th Century to the time of the First World War and John Maclean. In **Peter Scrimgeour**'s, 'I See the Salmon Flow', written specially for this book, we continue the course of that story, through the Second World War, then to the UCS work-in, obliquely referred to, and so to the present day. The French ship mentioned in the first verse is the *Maillé Brézé*, a destroyer, scuttled in 1940 by its crew after an accidental fire broke out, when the ship was stationed in the Clyde, off Greenock. It was widely believed that, in scuttling her, the crew saved many civilian lives on shore; but more than two dozen of the crew lost theirs.

'I See the Salmon Flow' is the latest of more than a hundred poems, lyric and narrative, that Peter Scrimgeour has written since his time as a student at Glasgow School of Art. For two summer seasons then, he worked as a purser on the Clyde steamers. Going 'doon the watter' so many times served to feed his visual imagination, and to give him a feel for the flow and history of the river. Another influence on the writing of 'I See the Salmon Flow', affecting the choice of verse-form and use of rhythm, is the poet's long immersion in folk songs, a favourite singer-songmaker being Eric Bogle.

After serving his time as an engineer with Babcocks and Wilcox in Renfrew, **George McEwan**, a native of Maybole, returned to Ayrshire, where he became a prime mover in establishing the Ayr Folk Club. Through this, he met various well-known figures in the folk revival, including Hamish Henderson, Ewan MacColl, Peggy Seeger, Martin Carthy, Tom Paley, Matt McGinn, Archie and Ray Fisher, Alex Campbell, Hamish Imlach, and Billy Connolly. It was after a meeting of the Club, as they sat swapping poems, that, in George

McEwan's own words, 'Billy became taken by a wee number titled "The Welly Boot Song." Later this resulted in *The Great Northern Welly Boot Show*.' After more than twenty years as Senior Technician in Stromness Academy, Orkney, George McEwan moved to Glasgow, where he is active as a member of various writers' groups. A number of his poems and short stories are to be found on the Maybole website www.maybole.org.

'Ballad for Upper Clyde', written in August, 2010, and published here for the first time, tells the story of the UCS work-in, taking it from initial feelings of despair, then anger, then defiance (conveyed in an exchange of dialogue), through to the mobilisation of action (conveyed in a documentary style), and so to a retrospective placing of the work-in in the context of Scottish history. New names are to be carved 'wi' respect an' honest pride' in the 'Ha' o' Heroes', to stand with 'The Wallace, Bruce, and unsung folk...' This powerful ballad gives poetic expression to the same conviction - that the UCS work-in is of lasting significance – that inspired the compiling of this book. Of course, as in all matters entailing politics, there are differences of opinion among our contributors. To what extent, for example, should the work-in be regarded as a Scottish and/or British and/or working class phenomenon? Not all our contributors – maybe not even two – would give the same answer. 'Ballad for Upper Clyde' is based 'loosely on an old folk song called "High Germanie". The lyrics seem to fit the tune as I remember it...'

In **Jackie Kay**'s 'The Shoes of Dead Comrades' we hear two voices, that of the poet herself, and, through her, her father's. We learn of 'dead comrades', honoured and fondly remembered, along with 'Everything they ever believed'. We march with them – against Polaris, for UCS – down through the years, and into the future. We are made aware of mortality, and of continuity, too. The father who is central to this poem is John Kay, formerly a full-time organiser for the Communist Party of Great Britain in Scotland. Like many elegies, this beautiful poem combines celebration and commemoration with its note of mourning.

Jackie Kay is Professor of Creative Writing at Newcastle University. Her published works include poems e.g. *The Adoption Papers* (1991), novels e.g. *Trumpet* (1998), and short stories e.g. *Wish I Was Here* (2006). A recent 'autobiographical journey', *Red Dust Road* (2010), movingly demonstrates the truth of its motto text, 'The past is never past.' Her answer to the question, 'Why bother with poetry?', put to her in The Poetryclass Interview (The Poetry Society, 2001), more than justifies the publication of this book and others like it. It makes the following strong points: 'Poetry is language at its most rich... Poetry inhabits ideas better than any other form... Poetry stands the test of time.'

In our Introduction, the literary and political significance of our title, *A Rose Loupt Oot*, is explained. Its optimistic imagery – taken from the section of Hugh MacDiarmid's *A Drunk Man Looks at the Thistle* that celebrates the initial upsurge of The General Strike of 1926 – is quoted, and expanded upon. If we read further in MacDiarmid's masterpiece, however, we soon come to lines where a different imagery prevails: 'Syne the rose shrivelled suddenly / As a balloon is burst.' The Drunk Man interprets this collapse according to a stern doctrine, as much theological as political: 'The vices that defeat the dream / Are in the plant itsel'...'

The trajectory described by the poems in *A Rose Loupt Oot* is not so falling and fading, we trust, as that described by the bloom on The Drunk Man's thistle. Our poets combine to offer some hope that 'The dream o' beauty' that inspired the popular struggles of the past, including the UCS work-in, is 'derning yet / Ahint the ugsome shape' of its constraining forces.

Ballad of the Red Clyde

Come all ye fake historians
and hiders of the Truth,
my story I will tell to you,
and starting with my youth!
Beneath the mossy Lowther Hills,
my journey does begin,
on winding thro the Lanark glades
and doon by Orra Linn.

I nurtured all those sylvan shades
where peasants tilled their fields,
and many a pleasant Autumn hairst
those crops o' bounty yield;
on sun-lit streams and silver gleams,
I roam so wild and free
'til I join the tide
of the estuary wide
and dance into the sea.

I saw the Glasgow fishermen
their little shielins build,
I saw the lairds deprive them
o' the very lands they tilled;
I saw the poor gaunt weaving folk
all toiling night and day,
their weary sleep, their struggle deep,
their lives o' hodden grey.

I saw the Lanark miners
a similar fate endure,
the smelters doon by Waukenfield,
these legions of the poor,
and when they 'rose in protest deep,
to me 'twas no surprise,
for old Clyde had seen, baith morn and e'en,
the anguish in their eyes.

The cruel bosses on my banks
no pity had nor shame;
with sword and gun at dead o' night
their hired troops all came,
and I wept to see such agony,
the sorrows and the loss
when they chained old 'Pearly' Wilson
and hanged him at the Cross.

I loaned my streams to Glasgow's poor,
my girth made deep and wide
'til I became in song and fame
the bonny river Clyde;
the riveters and caulker lads,
they sang in praise of me,
and waves that washed the anvilled yards
stirred yearnings to be free.

'Til there arose upon my banks
a stalwart breed of men,
who vowed that they would never be
poor suffering slaves again;
with dignity and courage stood,
nor did they stand in vain!
What joy to me to live to see
The likes of John Maclean.

Their emblem was the banner red,
they were no craven crew;
like Clyde has served you with its streams,
they lived and fought for you.
Their tribe still live throughout the years,
nor change with Time nor Tide!
For Liberty come sing with me
this ballad of the Clyde.

Freddy Anderson

from A Clydeside Lad

X

Darkir yit on midnight's darkniss,
like the shaddy o a monster,
stauns the night shape o the shipyerd,
beast o steel an stane an timber.

Droonin stars wae floods o fire,
broodin noo, noo breathin thunder,
earth's a-shudder wae its power,
power tae meld an power tae sunder.

Iron-bodied, iley-blidded,
black Leviathin in labour,
waarm within its womb o girders
sleeps the beauty o a liner.

Fed fat wae the sweat o workers,
fodder fur its belly's abyss,
dragon o ma chilthood's windae,
whit god's, whit divvil's beast is this?

XIX

Ther's moss an dock an grass in dibbits,
    the odd strang daisy tae,
graun oot this grimy shipyerd waw
    Thit locks me in the day.

Ma Da an uncles spoke fur me;
    they said nae lad wis finer;
sae here Ah staun on ma furst day,
    a new apprentice jiner.

The roar o rivets, screech o cranes,
    the groan an grind o gear
hiv numbed ma lugs an numbed ma brain
    bit cannae numb ma fear.

An up ower ther ten thousand men
    made smaw agen the hull,
swarm like dark bees aboot a hive
    or ants upon thir hill.

Ma fear tells me thit in this place
    a soul cid lose itsel -
oh God, if only Ah cid wake
    an find Ah'd dreamt o Hell.

Fur nowt thit's weak or frail, Ah know,
    cin flourish in this place,
an wurdliss ma hert begs release –
    or else fur iron grace.

Bit yit high up yon mucky waw
    Ah see a floor is bloomin,
a sign tae say thit folk cin thole
    this Hell an still stay human.

Ootside this store noo gruff big men
    grin ower an dunt thir mate
is Ah staun here where Ah've been sent
    Tae get 'a guid, lang weight'.

XXV

Her mooth wis fuul o chuckie-stanes –
'God bless this ship and all who sail...'
an we wir laughin wild is wains
it muck on oor yerd-owner's tail
fae where he'd slipt on ile and fell,
the day we launched the San Miguel.

The botil smashed. Ther came a hush
sae lang an wide it felt like noise,
tae wee Joe yellt, 'It wants a puush!'
then, like it waited fur his voice,
the Giant edged oot fur the swell,
the day we launched the San Miguel.

A roar rose up sae strang an fierce,
loud fit tae crack the cranes above,
an many throats choked many tears
bit nane cid hide the powerfa love
thit burnt in awe, is in masel,
the day we launched the San Miguel.

Pride ran sae deep it near wis pain
an me, ma fethir bae ma side,
watched whit oor hauns hid built, oor ain,
the ocean noo take fur its bride,
an take fae us pert o oorsel,
the day we launched the San Miguel.

Ther's men drag coal up oot the mine,
ther's men drag rhymes up oot thir soul,
ther's men build buildins, taw an fine,
bit in this big, crule, sweaty hole
we built a beauty oot a Hell,
the day we launched the San Miguel.

Bill Sutherland

POWER TO THE PEOPLE

with love from JOHN AND YOKO

AUGUST 9TH 1971

Struggle

Not to certainly means
worsening conditions
inevitable defeat.

To engage in action
even if you lose
means dignity at least.

It also means
just could mean
that you actually win.

But it's more than that
for in the process
people change.

They awaken and grow
like desert seeds
receiving rain.

And give to others
a sense of vision
and possible dreams.

Jim Aitken

Counting

' the moneychangers are still with us... Far from being reviled,
they are very pillars of the establishment...' (Jimmy Reid,
'Christianity and Communism', 1975)

those who count
                can count
and those who don't count
                don't

now the counters want to invent
a way of counting what can't be counted

the counters need counters
to account for the uncountable

it gets them back to square one

meanwhile those who don't count
don't count on it

they count themselves lucky

there's nothing to it really

Tessa Ransford

from Glasgow Sonnets

V

'Let them eat cake' made no bones about it.
But we say let them eat the hope deferred
and that will sicken them. We have preferred
silent slipways to the riveters' wit.
And don't deny it – that's the ugly bit.
Ministers' tears might well have launched a herd
of bucking tankers if they'd been transferred
from Whitehall to the Clyde. And smiles don't fit
either. 'There'll be no bevvying' said Reid
at the work-in. But all the dignity you muster
can only give you back a mouth to feed
and rent to pay if what you lose in bluster
is no more than win patience with 'I need'
while distant blackboards use you as their duster.

Edwin Morgan

'I worked in the Clydebank Division of the UCS as a wages clerk. The work-in at
UCS was a wonderful and inspiring period in my life. I was one of the first to be
paid off by the liquidator (September, 1971), and was re-employed by the work-in's
Coordinating Committee the following day. I was given the responsibility of
handling the wages of the men and women who were re-employed by the
Committee. You must remember the work-in had received messages of support
and financial contributions from the British public, trade unions, and many other
organisations and individuals, and also from overseas. These were tremendous
contributions financially and morally. We felt that society was on our side, and
they knew that what was happening on Clydeside – with the Tory Government's
attempt to close us down – was wrong, and was not based on the actual facts at
that time. I will never forget the generosity shown to the UCS workers.'
Isabel Dickie

Cartoon by Bob Starrett

an còmhlachd

nuair a mhaoidh iad pasgadh
chuir sinn romhainn a bhi strì
ann an làraich ar buinn
aig gach uidheam is inneal,
's ma liùg iomagain idir mar
chnuimh tromh na féithean,
dh'éirich guth
    agus chuala sinn
(mar gum bẽ soidheach
a' cur saidh ri cuan corrach)
tagradh air sgiathan cothroim
gu siùbhlach a' sealltainn
    dealbh dhuinn de
dh'abhainn bheò threòirean
sìos gu cuan nan teachdraidh
far nach bàthar buil
    nan seasadh sinne
mar ruighe sgeirean
    tromh nach sàthadh
spaileart spreadhach
    am fuathan caomha
d' ar bith is iarrtas
    airson còir is ceartas

anns an fhoireann sìtheil
an aghaidh nam murtair mall
a mhùchadh ar n'anail fhéin
dhearbh sinn lìomh ar stuth
agus sheas, agus sheas

bha 'n abhainn ud na bratach
leathann, suaicheantas
    sìor-shiùbhlach do
shaothair chruaidh na shìolaich
air a bruaichean –
    miadhail dhuinne
na gàraidhean móra far nach

in unison

when they threatened folding
we agreed to resist
just where we stood
at each tool and machine
and if any maggots of doubt
should creep through our sinews
a voice arose
              and we heard
(as if a vessel were
addressing prow to precipitous ocean)
an appeal on wings of justice
eloquently sketching
              for us the shape of
a living stream of energies
down to the ocean of futures
where outcomes cannot be drowned
              if we stand
like a ridge of reefs
              that can't be pierced
by the explosive torpedo
              of their bland hatred
of our being and need
              for rights and justice

as a peaceful brigade
against those slow murderers
who'd strangle our very breath
we proved our mettle's strength
and we stood, and we stood
that river was a broad
banner, an ever –
              supple emblem of
the hard labour that bred
on its banks –
              esteemed by us
the great yards where neither

fàsadh feur no flùr,
        far an sgaoileadh iadsan
siùil dubha luibheach
                an nàimhdeas
far an togadh iad fàsach

ach seall, na soidhichean
dhan tug sinn loinn,
                faic moit nan meur
a rinn an lainnreach
faic an druim nach diùlt cromadh
                ri ceann-uidhe
a' togail buaidh

Aonghas MacNeacail

grass nor bloom could grow,
          where those would scatter
the black weed sails
                    of their malice
where they'd raise a desert

but see, the ships
we gave a finish,
                    see the pride of fingers
that gave them grace
see a back not afraid to stoop
                    toward objective
erect in triumph

Aonghas MacNeacail

Banner and Roses

*'I gave birth to my daughter in the maternity ward of the
Southern General, and that's where John and Yoko's flowers
ended up, and they were spread well over'.* (Pat Milligan)

It's a long march to where I hope we're going.
It's many years away, and many changes
to our lives; but first, for now,
we'll stop at Glasgow Green.
That's far enough today.

Mind you hold your end of the banner high,
and firm, against this stiff wind blowing!
Can the words be seen:
our claim of right, our call for unity,
our plea to the world to join our fight?
Yes? Good! They're readable,
stretched tight.
Feel how the banner bucks,
like a red sail swelling!
Bright as a beacon, it's our hope's proof,
our strength's telling.

Did you hear of the flowers we got,
an armful of roses, with a cheque,
from John and Yoko, some while back?
That rose bush that we passed –
by the park gate there – reminded me.

Imagine:
from our black trades, from our yards,
we touched the two of them;
we moved them;
gave their hearts' heart a shove.
Like us, they're on a march,
long and winding.
Like us, they wonder why in the world
there's greed, and why there's hunger.

Our ways crossed;
the common factor,
love.

We sent their roses on,
to a mother-and-baby ward.
We spread them wide:
one bloom at least at every bed.
Let the first gift that the new-born get,
we thought, be these shared flowers.
Never mind the babies' eyes, unfocused,
could not see their deep red;
their mothers' did.

Hold your end of the banner high,
and hold it firm,
against the wind's blowing.
We want our words seen, and spread,
from here, from Glasgow Green,
a red flood flowing.

David Betteridge

I am the *Esperance*

Gerda Stevenson

I am the *Esperance*, I sail in your wake,
canvas unfurled, bellied with hope
as you pour into Glasgow Green –
we are your chorus, my sisters and I,
your creation, a fleet of belief, heading back to the Clyde
from the seven seas: veteran *Hikitia*, floating crane,
the only one of her kind in the world, she's home again
from Wellington; and *Empire Nan*, our stout tug;
Delta Queen – her great stern wheel churns the foam
as she steams in from the Mississippi; and bold *Akasha*,
laden with memories of the Nile; we shimmer for you,
our riggings clink, our funnels boom to your cry:
'The Right To Work, Not a Yard Will Close,
Not a Man Down the Road,' your banners and flags
like waves before us, drawing us home in one great tide;
Umoja's here, her name bearing our purpose today –
unity – a gleam on her prow; *Moonstone* and *Seva*,
who well as any know all about salvage –
and there's *Uhuru*, named for freedom,
Uhuru, Uhuru, my sister Uhuru, sailing with me
in your wake, my canvas unfurled, freighted with hope,
as wave upon wave, you surge into Glasgow Green.

At the UCS Work-in

The workers were supported
with impromptu dinner time shows
in the canteen where they sat at long bench tables
eating from bowls
like extras in an Oliver Twist movie.

Today, a man dressed in a leopard-skin leotard
stood on top of such a table,
squatted slightly with hands
gripping his knees
as a comrade clamped
what looked like
a giant piece of elastic between leotard man's teeth.

The comrade proceeded
to walk the length of the canteen
and as the elastic stretched
he informed us all
that what leotard man had in his mouth
was heavy duty industrial knicker elastic,
that, when released,
would travel at a velocity of 100 mph
and smash into leotard man's face
with a force of 100 lbs per square inch.

When the comrade stopped at the top end of the canteen,
the knicker elastic taut above the diners' heads,
with leotard man grimacing
with the elastic clenched in tightly shut jaws,

his comrade asked, 'Are – you – ready?'

Leotard man replied, 'Yes!'

at which the elastic
whipped across the heads of diving diners,
all wearing smiles of survival.

Tomorrow,
on the same table
there would be a basket
of red roses from John & Yoko –
an altogether more peaceful affair.

Brian Whittingham

'That struggle would have been birds flying on one wing if the women had not
been involved. They were at the heart of the communities. The women – the
partners, the mothers, the lovers, the sisters, everybody – did it: they
transformed the struggle. They took imagination. They carried the baton
forward. It couldn't have happened without them.'
Pat Milligan

'Dear Shop Stewards,
Please find enclosed £2 p.o. (postal order) my school pals and I raised at a
street jumble sale in aid of the UCS workers. This was a hurried Jumble Sale
because we felt you would need the money to fight that bad man Mr. Heath
who is taking away your jobs.
We wish you well from Aberdeen.
John McConnachie (13)
Ronald Belsham (14)
Elaine McConnachie (10)

Clyde-built: the UCS

I

Marchers, banners, pipe-bands, this time
all Scotland fought a different war,
collections, petitions, the razzamatazz,
the people's cause, for once not just rhetoric,
the Tories and the Tory press caught,
gobsmacked, by the inventive audacity of,
not shiftless strikers, but four yards working,
making ships, with famous Clyde-built skill,
riveters, taking on a clique of London bankers,
Yanks, monopolists out to bring the Thirties
back, but no thanks, pal, not here, not yet,
not without a fight, this protest, this
burgeoning movement forming round the work-in,
the Churches, even John Lennon, attracted by
the upfront commonsense of 'the right to work',
Jimmy Reid's – 'there'll be no bevvying' – we
knew then that this would be no fool's paradise
but something real, for we heard them dragging
as they went their pride, bedraggled, arguing.

II

Liverpool, 1972, an end of placement party,
student social workers and community workers
having a farewell bash, *Brown Sugar* blaring
and I'm talking to some about the UCS until
this Goldsmith College Rastafarian smart-arse
starts giving out how Reid etcetera have sold
out the working-class, the Revolution, and thus
a furious disputation arose. Next time I saw him,
he as leader of Liverpool Council, Derek Hatton,
telly smart, the hair short, the smirk, the same
super sure certainty of the showroom salesman,
the eyes, still double-glazed, selling what he
called 'socialism' short, as would his soon to be
doppelganger, Tony Blair.

Alistair Findlay

The Industrial Relations Act, 1971 (Repealed 1974)

We were part of a big demonstration.
New St Andrew's House was jam-pack';
the Tories' Industrial Relations –
the dole and a knife in the back.

Then up gets Michael McGahey
to a roar that near halted the band.
First he dealt with a few class illusions,
then he says with a sweep of his hand:

'They're going to jail now your trade union leaders,
to frighten you out of courage,
but, as I said to my friend here, Hugh Wyper,
what's "Life" to a man of his age?'

We sang till our roofs hit the rafters,
we swelled up and swelled up with joy.
McGahey had Ted Heath for afters,
like a dog has a wee squeaky toy.

Alistair Findlay

Cartoon by Bob Starrett

Showing a Way

'We are witnessing an eruption not of lava but of labour. The labour of working men and women...' (Jimmy Reid, Glasgow Green, 18 August, 1971)

Once upon a time – here,
in the real world, for this is not a fairy tale –
a bold idea changed *If* to *That*.
Imagine, acted on by many,
took on the force of hard material fact.
This happened forty years ago;
the place, the shipyards of the Upper Clyde.
The wonder is, given the world's wounds since,
the bold idea has not yet died.

All rivers have their storied past,
in part the same, in part unique.
More than a few have known the pride
of ships well made and safely launched;
and also known, when fortunes ebb,
a shadow-side. But here, at UCS,
a Labour victory was ours;
and Capital, out-classed, endured reversal,
and a loosening of its powers.

The reason is not hard to seek:
big on any scale, a volcano, not of lava
but of Labour, burst in flame. The action
that eight thousand shipyard workers took
filled the bright skies of politics. Briefly,
social order's deep assumptions shook.
That is the core of Clyde's especial claim.

Lame duck, said Capital, dismissive
and devaluing of the yards.
Never mind the lives invested there,
the teeming skills, the order book!

Never mind the hinterland they served,
that equally in turn served them!

Dead duck was what it wished to see,
little knowing that our bird would fly,
and soar, deriving strength from thousands,
then from tens of thousands more.

Unite and fight! In tandem, and in full,
heeding the maxim's dual elements,
not from the dole outwith the shipyards' gates,
but working from within: there
lay the workers' stratagem,
that helped us win.

The shipyards' mail bag,
like a farmer's sack of seed, spilled out
its daily bulge of contents: news received
of rallies, demonstrations, strikes;
well-wishers' words, and sometimes flowers;
and cash, from corner shops, from churches,
children, unions, and the whole wide listening world,
sums both large and widows' generous mites –
sent in comradeship, to keep
the struggle's fire alight.

The yards were saved: the bold idea,
in act, had proved its worth.
But now, four decades on, what's left?
In place of gain, a creeping dearth.
Not only ships have sunk, or gone for scrap,
but yards as well, and jobs, and skills,
and with them, hope. Along the river,
as throughout the land, and world,
we feel a cutting wind that kills.
Economic winter has us in its grip.

For Capital, the battle that it lost in '71
was clarion-call and school;
it learned far more than we.
It learned to hone its tools of shock,

displace, lay off, and rule.
Ganging up and doing down,
it made too many of us settle, first for slices
of the loaf we made, then beggars' crusts,
then bugger all. Ruthlessly,
it grabbed again its habitual crown.

For us, a tragedy ensued,
its playing-out still under way:
comrades at loggerheads and each others' throats;
lost sense of purpose and of common cause,
confusion and the side-track having won the day;
unions and parties pulled apart, offering least,
not best resistance in a losing war.
What should – what could – we have attempted
otherwise, or more?
Can we combine to build afresh that bold idea
that found expression and a home at UCS?
Can we re-launch it on the carrying stream
of people's wants and dearest dreams?
Can we extend it to the point it captures
greater powers, and thus rebuts,
with allies everywhere,
the might that Capital will bring to bear?

The world shifts restlessly; a rising flood
of tremors agitates beneath; fresh rifts
in what we thought was solid mass appear.
Deep energy demands release.
Eruptions can't be far: the forecast's clear.

Present struggle cries to know
the complex story of its past. Take it!
Save it from erasure, or revision's grasp!
What happened here in '71
can be no Terra nullius of the mind, open
for errors to invade. It's where,
ablaze and wise, we entered history,
and showed a way whereby a future
might be made.

David Betteridge

The Titan Crane

sits beside the empty dock,
with only its coat of blue paint
to shield it from the Clydeside wind
that licks the flattened debris that was the yard.

A small bus winds its way along the dockside
to the crane that's now a tourist attraction.

Inside, a spattering of passengers –
An ex-welder now living in California,
his brother, an ex-plater, now living in Dublin
and two other brothers, born and bred Bankies,
an ex-rigger and an ex-burner and their wives.

A lift silently ascends with the family
to a steel mesh platform 150 ft. in the air
that gives them a bird's-eye view of desolation.

In the jib's machine room
the gears and wires and wheels
of the once mighty crane
are still and silent and dead.

Apart from the whining wind,
the only sound comes from the flat-screen
that shows a celluloid shipyard
full of industry and noise and life.

The brothers and wives watch,
arms linked round each other's shoulders.

Outside they wander round the jib-deck
looking at the remnants of the end of the slipways
still poking their toes into the Clyde
where the great liners each made
an introductory bow towards Snodgrass field.
The wives see a barren panorama
of rubble and nothingness.

The brothers see ghosts of sprouting hulls
traversed by workers like boiler-suited ants,
and they hear a shrill horn piercing the air
and the clatter of thousands of steel-toe capped boots
worn by spectres stampeding towards the gates.

Brian Whittingham

'The British trade union movement, right up to the TUC, was mobilised in
solidarity. It is difficult to convey the atmosphere of the British people and
beyond internationally. At the two major demonstrations in Glasgow, there
were spontaneous stoppages in all kinds of industries. Workers just walked out.
I vividly remember the women from Wills tobacco factory singing their own
songs all the way.'
John Kay

'Writer Carl MacDougall phoned yesterday re other matters. I mentioned UCS
and he told me the following tale. He was down at the work-in, and chatting to
writer Archie Hind. Gus MacDonald and a TV film crew were filming. A man
carrying a plank stopped and spoke to the crew, then went on. Gus came over
to Carl and Archie to share what the plank-carrier had said. It was at the time
that the reputedly fairly pornographic film I Am Curious Yellow was getting
much publicity. The plank-carrier said he had a suggestion for the film crew,
that their film should be titled "I Am Furious Red".'
Ewan McVicar

Something Like Grief

She'd come from her father's funeral,
her rayon dress too thin for the weather.
She walked on past the shipyard
where he'd worked those forty years.
She walked on past the banners
as she did now every evening
coming home from the bakery.
'Not a Yard Will Close,' they shouted,
'Not a Man Down the Road'.

She walked on past the pub
but stopped when she heard the music.
A fiddler played a reel
then voices sang a workers' anthem,
all out of tune and out of time
and lustily defiant,
while in the smoky air, thick with hope,
the riveters turned managers
planned next week's production.

She recalled her father's promise,
the Big Girl bike she'd yearned for,
pink with silver tassels.
She'd have it for her birthday –
until the whipround in the pub,
this pub,
when Dave MacPherson's wife
was made a widow in the yards.

It was then she heard the singer,
indistinct against the traffic,
till a red light let her listen.
A voice of pure and perfect clarity
rose and fell and crested
through the waves of 'Ol' Man River'.

As she listened, night was falling,
her rayon dress a flag unfurling
in the shadow of the shipyard,
and though she couldn't name the feeling,

it was something like grief,

it was something like joy.

Donna Franceschild

'There's a lot of feeling about among the women folk. They feel as strongly about the close down of Upper Clyde Shipbuilders as the men because it affects the whole future of their entire families. They know as much, if not more, just what the closedown will mean to the community...'
Joan Reid

U.C.S. Production up 87% with a reduction in manpower of 25%.
Yes John I think that qualifies as a lame-duck.

Cartoon by Bob Starrett

Clearances: a Diptych

I   Redemption

From Dornoch we moved further north,
not as north as where she was born
but north enough to understand;
to understand her returning.
She sat there beneath the sculpture
of 'The Emigrants' at Helmsdale,
moved by the woman looking back
to the strath that was once her home.
For she too once had to leave here
to work in service or in shops;
she too, with some eighty years now,
lived in the south and not the north.
And these years have moved her to tears
and this woman brought them all back,
yet she sits with son and daughter
who marvel at her dignity.
Two highland ladies, one in bronze,
and the other in flesh that pains,
bestow upon a changing world
unchanging values that redeem.

II   Clyde-Built

Once they threw us off our lands
made us sail the stormy seas
or scavenge along sea shores
beneath the tall dark cliffs
and still they made us fight their wars.

We came south in search of work
leaving the fresh smell of the heather
and the smell of burning peat
behind us as scents that had vanished
and still they made us fight their wars.

Maclean, McShane, Gallacher and Maxton
became our new clan chiefs, better than before
and we marched with them, our banners high
and the pipers played out at the front
as the Highlands and Lowlands combined.

Their legacy and the legacy of Davitt
came together too with Reid and Airlie
and Sammy Barr, as we worked on instead
showing a brand new kind of human dignity,
a Clyde-built face; built down all these ages.

And we need no memorial along these banks
because one exists already and stands proud
on the Clyde with her arms raised high
to the heavens. And we stood like La Pasionara,
inspired by her, refusing to go on our knees.

Jim Aitken

Drawing by Bob Starrett

Jaggily

for Bob Starrett

Friend, your bramble's thorns are sharp
as sharp. Whoever thinks to pick the fruit –
your drawing makes the point -
will run the risk of hurt.
As well as thorns, and leaves,
your penwork's densities of black on white
convey the thickened stems of older growth
in stark, dark contrast to the new.
Stiff now, and hard to push aside,
they give the tendrils of fresh green
a palisade of strength,
and skyward pathways to pursue.

This sketch you've sent
I've pinned on my study wall. There,
with Luxemburg close by, and Spartacus, and Parks,
and those who breached the Winter Palace gates,
and all the folk of UCS, and John Maclean
above, your bramble clambers
jaggily.

A comfort and discomfort,
it's a spur to action in the cause –
unfinished, but continuing –
that we, along with millions, love
and cannot help but love,
implacably.

David Betteridge

He Wouldn't Want an Elegy

in memory of a veteran of the UCS Work-in

and as for poetry
he'd want it plain

he'd want it plain and simple
and outspoken as the rain

he wouldn't want it dressed up
in a party frock of words
with lots of frilly metaphors
he'd want it to be heard

he'd want it writing slogans
of solidarity
with men who honour labour
and fight for Unity

he'd want it kicking arses
of the mob who make the rules
who starve and maim and plunder,
put power in hands of fools
he'd want it bold as thunder
and outspoken as the rain

he'd want it
marching, marching
on the citadels of power
he'd want to hear it roar
against greed and its profanity
ROAR until all humanity
joins hands in solidarity
with eyes as sharp as lightning
with voices bold as thunder
and dancing in the rain

Chrys Salt

Fresh Chapters

The Titan Crane, Clydebank

Industry gone,
Decay, decline,
A town upon its knees;
Towards the river, towards the skies,
The Titan stands amid the breeze.

Queens grew up
Beneath her gaze,
Giants of the waters.
The Titan protects the town that was
And all her sons and daughters.

The town,
Born on the Banks o' Clyde,
Remnant of another age;
In stubborn hope, her people write
Fresh chapters, page by page.

Now ghost ships
Glide through the early dawn,
Horns welcoming in New Year;
The Titan of the future,
Banishes all fear.

She towers above the Clyde,
Unbroken and unbowed;
A symbol of the past,
Reborn,
She takes her place with pride.

Danny McCafferty

I See the Salmon Flow

Forward flowed my history,
From peace the world turned.
War saw my water flaming red
As I watched while Clydebank burned.
To save Greenock from disaster,
I felt French sailors die;
But in their rusting hulk
Their memories still lie.

I saw shipbuilding dying,
Till men began to fight
To stop the closing of the yards,
Showing solidarity is might.
People came together
With their passion and their pride.
I felt at one with them
And proud to be the Clyde.

Once ships from many lands
Used my mighty docks.
Now stand exhibition centres
And yuppie flats in blocks.
But my water now is cleaner
And fear begins to go.
I feel the water fresher
And I see the salmon flow.

Peter Scrimgeour

Ballad for Upper Clyde

Ach Peggy lass, ach Peggy, pit mah workin boots away
An' don't lay oot mah biler suit for ah'll no' work the day.
The hammers they are silent, the welds are getting caul'
An' ower aw the shipyairds ye can hear the silence fall.
Nae mair the mighty ships o' steel will sail oot faur an' wide.
They've sent the Liquidator in tae murder Upper Clyde.

But, Wullie love, Oh Wullie, the news is gaun the roons
That there's a michty steer aboot doon at the gates at Broon's.
The stewards hae met the gether wi' the lads that goat their cairds.
They've thrown the Liquidator oot, they've occupied the yairds.
Wi' Jimmy Reid an' Airlie, they've made the Tyrants reel,
An' Heath an' aw his cronies shall taste oor Iron Heel.

The workers o' the Clydeside hae rallied tae the cry,
Men an' weemen aw determined no' tae let their livin' die.
This damned humiliation's the straw that broke the camel's back.
Enough, enough, we've had enough; this time we're fightin' back.
Naw, no' wi' swords or spears or guns, but wi' oor hauns an' sweat.
We'll show them how it should be done; we'll beat the bastards yet.

An' so the fecht went oan they days, remember them wi' pride,
The workin' men an' weeman whae strove tae rescue Upper Clyde.
'Nae slackin', naw nae bevvyin'!' Reid's challenge it was clear,
An' tae a man they laugh alood an' rally when they hear
Wi' baith Jimmys, Reid and Airlie, an' support frae roon the World,
At the bosses feet in prood defiance the Gauntlet it was hurled.

Noo mony years hae been an' gaun; they days are in the past.
The names lie in the Ha' o' Heroes; in memory they're cast,
The gallant few who Alba's freedom socht an' fearless took the lead,
The Wallace, Bruce, and unsung folk of whom we never read.
Noo tae that list o' fechtin' men whae strove baith lang an' fairly,
Carve wi' respect an' honest pride the names,
    Jimmy Reid an' Airlie.

George McEwan

The Shoes of Dead Comrades

On my father's feet are the shoes of dead comrades.
Gifts from the comrades' sad red widows.
My father would never see good shoes go to waste.
Good brown leather, black leather, leather soles.
Doesn't matter if they're a size too big, small.

On my father's feet are the shoes of dead comrades.
The marches they marched against Polaris. UCS.
Everything they ever believed tied up with laces.
A cobbler has replaced the sole, the heel.
Brand new, my father says, look, feel.

On my father's feet are the shoes of dead comrades.
These are in good nick. These were pricey.
Italian leather. See that. Lovely.
He always was a classy dresser was Arthur.
Ever see Wullie dance? Wullie was a wonderful waltzer.

On my father's feet are the shoes of dead comrades.
It scares me half to death to consider
that one day it won't be Wullie or Jimmy or Arthur,
that one day someone will wear the shoes of my father,
the brown and black leather of all the dead comrades.

Jackie Kay

Throw in the towel Prime Minister this one is going the distance.

Cartoon by Bob Starrett

Cartoon by Bob Starrett

Further Reading

John Foster

Two first-hand accounts were published while the work-in was still in force. The first, Alasdair Buchan's *The Right to Work*, Calder and Boyars, 1972, was based on Buchan's inside knowledge as a sympathetic journalist reporting for the Scottish and British press. The second, Willie Thompson and Finlay Hart, *The UCS Work-In* (Lawrence and Wishart, 1972) reflected Finlay Hart's experience as senior adviser to the stewards. Previously a shipyard convener himself and Communist Party industrial organiser, Hart was at that time a member of the Communist group on Clydebank Town Council. Alex Murray, as Scottish Secretary of the Communist Party, published *UCS - the Fight for the Right to Work*, in September 1971. Three other accounts were published in the immediate aftermath of the struggle. Jack McGill, *Crisis on the Clyde* (Davis-Poynter, 1973), provides the take of a *Daily Express* journalist; Stephen Johns, *Reformism on the Clyde* (Plough Press, 1973), that of the Workers Revolutionary Party; and Frank Broadway, *Upper Clyde Shipbuilders* (Centre for Policy Studies, 1976) that of the right-wing of the Conservative Party.

Autobiographical reflections can be found in Jimmy Reid, *Reflections of a Clyde-Built Man*, (Souvenir Press, London,1976) and Tony Benn, *Office Without Power: Diaries 1968-72* (Hutchinson, London, 1988). From the government side, Edward Heath, *The Course of My Life* (Coronet, London 1999) puts the blame on Nicholas Ridley. Jock Bruce-Gardyne, the PPS to the Scottish Secretary Gordon Campbell, attributes the government's retreat to fear of civil disorder in *Whatever Happened to the Quiet Revolution?* (Knight, London, 1974).

Academic studies are provided by John Foster and Charles Woolfson, *The Politics of the Upper Clyde Work-In: Class Politics and the Right to Work* (Lawrence and Wishart, 1986) and 'How Workers on the Clyde Gained the Capacity for Class Struggle: The Upper Clyde Shipbuilders Work-in 1971-72', in

J. McIlroy, *British Trade Unions and Industrial Politics*, vol 2 (Aldershot 1999). Brian Hogwood's *Government and Shipbuilding: the Politics of Industrial Change* (Saxon House, Farnborough, 1979) analyses the policy background and contains interviews with relevant government ministers. Chik Collins, *Language, Ideology and Social Consciousness* (Ashgate, 1999) analyses the stewards' use of language. Jim Phillips, *The Industrial Politics of Devolution: Scotland in the 1960s and 70s* (Manchester University Press, Manchester, 2008) reproduces the newly available archive materials from the Scottish Office and government departments in Westminster. His analysis stresses the long term significance of the work-in for changes in national attitudes to devolution and the role of the trade union movement.

Recent Scottish histories are somewhat uneven in their coverage. Tom Devine's *Scottish Nation 1700-2007* (Penguin, 2006) presents the work-in as an important and successful intervention by workers on the general issue of employment and economic development; Michael Lynch's coverage of the 1970s in *Scotland: A New History* (Century, London, 1991) makes no mention of it. Christopher Harvie dismisses the work-in as a 'publicity coup' in *No Gods and Precious Few Heroes: Scotland 1914-1980* (Edward Arnold, London, 1981); William Knox's *Industrial Nation: Work, Society and Politics in Scotland* (Edinburgh University Press, 1999) makes scant reference in his discussion of shipbuilding.

Two histories of the Scottish Trades Union Congress give the work-in a central place: Angela Tuckett, *History of the Scottish Trades Union Congress* (Mainstream, Edinburgh, 1987) and Keith Aitken, *Bairns o' Adam: the Story of the STUC* (Edinburgh, 1997)

There are two accounts of the 'Fairfield Experiment' at the Govan yard in the years immediately preceding the work-in: S. Paulden and B. Hawkins, *Whatever Happened at Fairfields?* (Gower Press, London, 1969) and the more authoritative study by Ken Alexander, who headed the STUC Inquiry in 1971, *Fairfields: A Study in Industrial Change* (Allen Lane, London,

1970). Bo Strath, *The Politics of De-Industrialisation: the Contraction of the Western European Shipbuilding Industry* (Croom Helm, 1987) sets the decline of the British shipbuilding industry in a wider setting. Jamie Webster and Russell Walker, *Back from the Brink* (Brown and Son, Glasgow, 2008) recounts the subsequent rescue of Govan yard in 1999.

The influence of the UCS on workplace occupations elsewhere is examined from an employers' perspective in Metra Consulting Group Ltd, *An Analysis of Sit-Ins* (Oxford, September 1972) and from a trade union viewpoint by North East Trade Union Studies Information Unit, *Workers Occupations* (Newcastle, 1976). Ken Coates, *Work-in Sit-ins and Industrial Democracy* (Spokesman, Nottingham 1981) seeks to relate the experience to the wider 'workers control' movement.

R. Hay and J. McLaughlan, 'The Oral History of Upper Clyde Shipbuilders', *Oral History*, vol. no. 1, 1973, provide an introduction to the materials in the Glasgow University archives. This collection also contains Jimmy Reid, *Alienation: Rectorial Address Glasgow University*, April 1972, and the UCS Joint Shop Stewards Committee Bulletins, Nos. 1-12 (1 September 1971 to 7 February 1972).

Glasgow Caledonian University Research Collections house varied archives and special collections relating to the Upper Clyde Shipbuilders work-in of 1971 and 1972. Material has been deposited from Bob Dickie and Jimmy Cloughley of the Co-ordinating Committee along with original artwork, bulletins, posters and cartoons all used as part of the campaign. Surviving records, photographs, published material and ephemera can be found in both the Communist Party of Great Britain Scottish Committee Archive and the Gallacher Memorial Library. The Scottish Trades Union Congress staged an enquiry into the proposed run-down of UCS and these records along with the STUC minutes and papers are kept as part of the Scottish Trades Union Congress Archive. They also hold the original exhibition THE RIGHT TO WORK: a celebration of the 30th anniversary of the UCS Work-in, created and staged by Govan Workspace at the time of the 30th anniversary.

Some useful websites:
www.bbc.co.uk/scotland/education/hist/employment
www.gcu.ac.uk/archives/ucs/
www.myclydebankphotos.co.uk

List of Illustrations

Page 19 *UCS* Drawing by Ken Currie, on loan to the STUC, Glasgow, reproduced by permission of the artist.

Page 28 *UCS* Preparatory sketch by Ken Currie for his People's History Paintings, Panel 7, displayed in The People's Palace, Glasgow, reproduced by permission of Culture and Sport Glasgow (Museums).

Page 39 Jimmy Reid addressing a meeting of shipyard workers at Linthouse, January, 1972. Photograph by Alex Young, from the Clydebank Library Collection, reproduced by permission of West Dunbartonshire Libraries and Museums Service.

Page 46 *Varda* and *Samjohn Pioneer* in the fitting out basin, John Brown's, 1972. Photograph by Alex Young, from the Clydebank Museum Collection, reproduced by permission of West Dunbartonshire Libraries and Museums Service.

Page 52 A mass meeting during the work-in. Photograph from the Clydebank Library Collection, reproduced by permission of West Dunbartonshire Libraries and Museums Service.

Page 60 Billy Connolly entertaining shipyard workers during the work-in. Photograph from the Clydebank Museum Collection, reproduced by permission of West Dunbartonshire Libraries and Museums Service.

Page 62 *Alisa* and *Varda* in the fitting out basin, John Brown's, 1972. Photograph by Alex Young, from the Clydebank Library Collection, reproduced by permission of West Dunbartonshire Libraries and Museums Service.

Page 80 The Titan Crane, 2010. Photograph by Owen McGuigan, reproduced with his permission.

Page 85 Notice advertising a benefit concert for the work-in, reproduced by permission of Glasgow Caledonian University Archives.

Page 91 Notice advertising a benefit concert for the work-in, reproduced by permission of Glasgow Caledonian University Archives.

Page 99 Card from John Lennon and Yoko Ono, accompanying their gift of roses and money made to the work-in, 9 August, 1971, reproduced by permission of Glasgow Caledonian University Archives.

Page 103 Cartoon by Bob Starrett, drawn for one of the Bulletins issued by the UCS Coordinating Committee, later published in *Rattling the Cage* (Ferret Press), reproduced by permission of the artist.

Page 115 Cartoon by Bob Starrett, drawn for one of the Bulletins issued by the UCS Coordinating Committee, later published in *Rattling the Cage* (Ferret Press), reproduced by permission of the artist.

Page 123 Cartoon by Bob Starrett, drawn for one of the Bulletins issued by the UCS Coordinating Committee, later published in *Rattling the Cage* (Ferret Press), reproduced by permission of the artist.

Page 126 *The Old and the New* Drawing by Bob Starrett, reproduced by permission of the artist.

Page 133 Cartoon by Bob Starrett, drawn for one of the Bulletins issued by the UCS Coordinating Committee, later published in *Rattling the Cage* (Ferret Press), reproduced by permission of the artist.

Page 134 Cartoon by Bob Starrett, drawn for one of the Bulletins issued by the UCS Coordinating Committee, later published in *Rattling the Cage* (Ferret Press), reproduced by permission of the artist.